FRIENDS
OF ACPL

UNDERSTANDING
PHOTOGRAPHY

UNDERSTANDING PHOTOGRAPHY

GEORGE SULLIVAN

Illustrated

FREDERICK WARNE & CO., INC.   NEW YORK & LONDON

ACKNOWLEDGMENTS

The author wishes to express his appreciation to Gary Wagner, president, Wagner-International Photos, Inc., New York, for his interest and cooperation in this project. Special thanks are also offered to Timothy Sullivan who posed for many of the pictures that appear herein.

CONTENTS

INTRODUCTION

The camera is one of the most amazing instruments ever invented, and in the past decade or so it has become even more amazing.

Compact, light-in-weight and incredibly versatile, present-day cameras do everything but point the lens and tell you when to shoot. Films have been so "speeded-up" that it's now possible to take pictures under conditions that were considered impossible not many years ago.

Yet despite the tremendous advances in cameras and film, photography is still much more than clicking the shutter. A photographer must understand the basic physical and chemical properties of cameras and film. He must know darkroom procedures.

Explaining photography in both its technical and creative aspects is the aim of this book.

UNDERSTANDING
PHOTOGRAPHY

On the slope of the moon's Hadley Delta, astronaut David R. Scott aims his 70 mm camera. (NASA)

chapter 1

THE CAMERA

When you point the front of your camera toward a subject and click the shutter, you set in motion a remarkable chain of events. An image of the subject is projected through the lens and onto the film. The film's light-sensitive coating, known as the *emulsion*, acts as a chemical memory, recording the image.

It is a "latent" image, however. You can't see it. It is something like holding your hands over your ears and watching Willie Mays whack a baseball. You know there's a sound but you can't hear it.

Developing is the process that renders the latent image visible. After the developing stage, then you have a *negative*, a kind of stencil, from which positive photographs, which are called *prints*, can be made.

You can come to a clearer understanding of this magical process by performing the experiments described in this and the next chapter. They're simple and inexpensive.

Let's begin with the camera. All cameras are the same, whether you are referring to the Kodak Instamatic camera you took along on your vacation trip or the sophisticated Hasselblad that Neil Armstrong packed along to the moon.

A camera is a lightproof box. Film is fixed at one end, while at the end opposite there is a *lens*, a small disk of optical glass that projects the image onto the film.

You can make a simple camera in a matter of minutes. Use a coffee can, the two-pound size. Paint the inside of the can with dull flat black enamel or lacquer. This is to minimize the possibility of reflecting light spoiling the experiment.

Using an awl, or a hammer and a nail, punch a small, well-rounded hole, not much larger than a pinhole, in the approximate center of the bottom of the can. Then wrap a piece of tissue paper or waxed paper around the open end of the can and secure it with a rubber band. (Figures 1 and 2.)

Figure 1.   Figure 2.

Take the camera outdoors. Holding the tissue paper end toward you, point the other end toward a brightly-lighted subject. The image of the subject will appear on the tissue paper. (You may have to enlarge the hole. You may also have to shield the tissue paper from stray light in order to obtain a strong image.)

Notice that the projected image is upside down. That's because light always travels in straight lines. So light from a point at the very top of your subject passes through the small hole to a point at the bottom of the image. The reverse happens in the case of light reflected from the bottom of the subject. It passes through the opening to a point at the top of the image. (Figure 3.)

Using the coffee-can viewer. (George Sullivan)

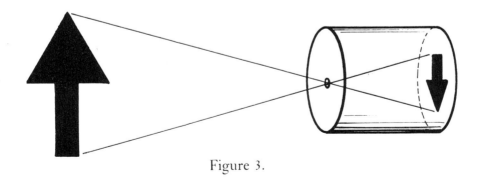

Figure 3.

The optical principle you see at work here has been known for centuries. Leonardo da Vinci, in notebooks he wrote in the 15th century, described such a device. He called it a *camera obscura*, Latin for "darkened chamber." Wrote da Vinci:

When the images of illuminated objects pass through a small round hole into a very dark room, if you receive them on a piece of white paper placed vertically in the room at some distance from the aperture, you will see on the paper all these objects in their natural shapes and colors. They will be reduced in size, and upside down, owing to the intersection of the rays at the aperture. If these images come from a place that is illuminated by the sun, they will seem as if painted on paper, which must be very thin and viewed from the back.

Artists, not photographers, were the first to put the *camera obscura* to practical use. They replaced the side facing the aperture with a pane of ground glass. It was then a simple matter to trace the projected image with brushes or crayons.

Artists gave practical use to the *camera obscura*.
(*Inspirations for Printers*; Westvaco Corporation)

14

The next step would seem obvious—to replace the ground glass with a sheet of light-sensitive material that could capture and retain the projected image. But this advance took centuries.

In 1800, Thomas Wedgwood, son of Josiah, the famous potter, performed experiments that pointed the way. He made a paper that was sensitive to light by coating it with silver salts. He then drew a picture on a pane of glass, placed it atop the sensitized paper, and exposed the two to sunlight. An image appeared on the paper. But Wedgwood was unable to fix the image, to make it permanent, after the glass was removed.

Nicephore Niepce, a French inventor, carried Wedgwood's work a step further. Using a paper coated with chloride of silver, Niepce was successful in capturing an image projected by a *camera obscura*. He also had some success in fixing the images by treating them with nitric acid.

Niepce's partner in experimentation was a French scenic artist named Louis J. M. Daguerre. A chance discovery helped Daguerre to develop concepts that were to immortalize his name. One day

Louis J. M. Daguerre.
(New York Public Library)

he put a plate that he had only partially exposed into a chemical storage cabinet. A few days later, when he returned to the cabinet to get the plate, he found there was a picture on the previously blank surface. Something in the cabinet had brought out the latent image. By trial and error experimentation, Daguerre found that it was mercury vapor that had caused the phenomenon.

This was a significant breakthrough. In all previous experiments photographers had been trying to produce a picture directly from the projected image. But Daguerre had stumbled upon the concept of developing the latent image *after* the film had been exposed. It is this principle upon which all photography of the present day is based.

In 1839 Daguerre announced the photographic process which came to be known as *daguerreotype*. It involved a plate sensitized by a coating of iodide of silver which was exposed to light. The image was then made permanent by a fixer consisting of mercury vapor and hyposulphite of soda.

Improvements quickly followed. William Henry Fox Talbot, a British inventor, developed a process to make positive prints from a negative. Frank Scott Archer contributed with the development of collodian and the "wet-plate" process, which was based on a glass negative.

The Daguerre system was not difficult to learn. Those who studied the instructional advice set down by Daguerre could become skilled cameramen. By the middle of the Nineteenth Century there were about ten thousand professional daguerro-typists in the United States.

The best known was Mathew Brady. To Brady's gallery on Broadway in New York City came the most eminent figures of the day to pose for portraits. Brady is remembered, however, for the pictorial record he made of the Civil War. He and his assistants photographed fortifications and military encampments, generals and

16

Brady's photograph of the wounded soldiers after the battle of Fredericksburg.
U.S. Signal Corps Photo (Brady Collection); National Archives

Brady's photographic outfit in the field. U.S. Signal Corps Photo (Brady Collection); National Archives

their staffs, and soldiers of both armies—dead and alive. But more than merely mirror his subjects, Brady captured the wretchedness of the war and its utter desolation. What he did is a landmark achievement in photography, seldom equaled and perhaps never surpassed.

Brady and his assistants had monumental technical problems to overcome. They used a wet-plate process, which meant that before a picture could be made a pane of glass had to be coated with collodion, a colorless, syrupy solution that reeked of alcohol. The plate then had to be treated with a solution of nitrate of silver and, while still wet, loaded into the big box camera. As soon as the picture was taken, the exposed plate had to be developed.

Brady and each of his men traveled in a wagon that served as a portable darkroom. It was also used to store the cameras, plates and assorted chemicals, and served as the man's living quarters as well.

During the 1870's, the wet-plate method was gradually superseded by the gelatin dry plate. In this, glass was coated with a gelatinous mixture of silver nitrate and cadmium bromide. Then the emulsion was allowed to dry. The advantage was that plates could be prepared ahead of time and used as needed. Dry plates were not only more convenient, they were fast. A photographer could snap a picture in 1/25 of a second.

Around the turn of the century, simple, portable box cameras came into general use. To a large extent these used a sensitized paper which could be printed with relatively simple equipment.

What really triggered photography's surge in popularity was the work of George Eastman, a manufacturer of dry plates in Rochester, New York. Eastman succeeded in coating long strips of paper with a light-sensitive emulsion and then he wound the strips on spools. A whole series of exposures could be made from a single spool. The convenience of Eastman's roll film led to millions becoming interested in photography.

18

This advertisement for "The Kodak Camera" appeared in 1889. (New York Public Library)

You can, with some slight modifications, adapt your coffee-can *camera obscura* so that it works in somewhat the same fashion as the early cameras of Daguerre, Brady and the others who pioneered the art and science of photography.

The first thing to do is to paint the can's plastic lid. Use the same black paint you used in painting the inside of the can. Paint both sides of the lid. After the paint is dry, be careful in handling the lid, for if any paint flakes off, the camera will no longer be lightproof.

The next step is to make a shutter to enable you to open and close the nail hole. Cut a 2×2½-inch flap out of stiff black paper. Tape it to the bottom of the can so that it is centered over the hole. You will have to use a second piece of tape along the bottom edge of the flap to hold it down firmly, locking out every bit of light. (Figure 4.)

Now for the film. Buy a roll of 120 or 620 Kodak Verichrome pan film. Working in total darkness, perhaps in a closet or the bathroom—some windowless room—unroll the film and cut it into 2½-inch squares. Tape one of the squares to the inside of the lid. This means that when the lid is in place the film will be positioned opposite the nail hole opening. (Figure 5.)

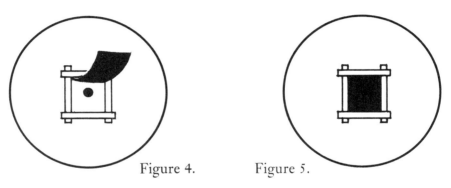

Figure 4.   Figure 5.

Be certain that the emulsion side of the film is facing the opening. It is the shiny side and slightly tacky when touched with moistened fingers. Be careful not to touch the film near the center. A fingerprint can ruin your work. Store the remaining film squares in a lighttight box.

Once the film is in place, clamp the lid on tightly. Be sure the shutter is closed tightly, too.

You must hold the camera perfectly motionless when you take your picture. It's best to place it on something firm, such as between two books lying flat on a table. Or you can tape it to a windowsill.

A photo taken with a pinhole camera. (Eastman Kodak Company)

The subject you choose must be in the sunlight. After aiming your camera, open the shutter. How long you leave it open depends on the condition of sunlight, whether it is bright sun or there is some cloudiness. In extremely bright sun, a two-second exposure may be sufficient. If there is some cloudiness, you may have to expose for as long as eight seconds.

Experiment. Without changing your subject, make several different exposures, varying the time from two to eight seconds.

Store the exposed squares of film in the lighttight box. The hidden, latent image that each bears is made visible through a two-stage process covered in the next chapter.

chapter 2

DEVELOPING and PRINTING

All of photography is based on the optical principle apparent in the *camera obscura* and the chemical principle that silver salts turn dark when exposed to light. In other words, clicking the shutter is only one-half of the photographic art. Processing the exposed film is the other.

Processing involves two steps—*developing* and *printing*, both of which take place in total darkness.

Developing is the process that converts the latent image into visible form. It involves immersing the film in a chemical bath known as the developer. This darkens the silver grains of the film emulsion, some more than others. The more light that has touched them, the faster they turn dark when subjected to the developing chemical. In areas of the film where no light has touched, no change takes place.

After being sloshed around in the developer, the film next goes into the fixer, or "hypo," an acid solution that washes away the undeveloped silver salts, leaving a fixed and permanent image.

Of course, you don't yet have a print. What you do have is a reverse, or "negative," image.

Printing is the process by which the negative is reversed to obtain true tonal values. The negative is placed in contact with, or its image projected onto, a piece of light-sensitive paper. Then the two are exposed to light. The transparent areas of the negative allow light to strike the paper and it turns black in the affected areas.

To do your own printing and developing, you need a temporary darkroom. The bathroom or kitchen will do. Each has a sink, running water and an electrical outlet, all of which are important to developing and printing. The kitchen is likely to have the added advantage of ample working space.

Make the room lighttight by covering the windows and cracks beneath the door. Lightproofing the room will be a good deal simpler if you work at night, for by simply pulling a shade you should be able to mask out stray light.

Determine whether the room is sufficiently dark by performing this test: Stay in the darkness for five minutes. At the end of the five minutes, if you can still see a sheet of white paper against a dark background, light is leaking in. Check for openings and cover them with black tape.

The simplest method is to process the film in trays. You need four trays. Special trays can be purchased in a photographic supply store but plastic or glass dishes will do. Each has to be somewhat larger than your film squares and at least two inches deep. Do not use metal containers, such as pie plates, unless they are stainless steel or enamelware.

You will also need a glass measuring cup, a thermometer, a glass stirring rod, a film clip—any simple spring clip will do—and a *safelight*, a special lamp equipped with one or more color filters capable of permitting moderate darkroom illumination.

You also will need three quart jars and a timer. A timepiece with a luminous face and sweep second hand is also adequate for timing.

Developing

Three chemicals are required for developing: the developer itself, a stop bath for rinsing, and a fixing bath, the hypo. Purchase the chemicals from a photographic equipment dealer. Be sure to explain your experiment to the salesperson, and ask his or her advice as to what type of chemicals you should purchase. Different types of films require different chemicals.

If the film you are developing is Kodak Verichrome pan film, it's economical to purchase the Kodak tri-chem pak. This contains the three chemicals you need and costs less than a dollar.

Label the three jars "Film Developer," "Stop Bath," and "Fixer." Mix the three solutions according to the directions on each package. After mixing, store each solution in its proper jar.

Be extremely careful in handling the chemicals. Even a few drops of stop bath or fixer can ruin the developer.

Arrange the four trays on a table in the darkroom. Keep them three or four inches apart. Working from left to right, pour developer into the first tray, stop bath into the second tray, and fixer into the third tray. Fill the fourth tray with water. Also place your timer on the table.

Before pouring the solutions from the jars into the appropriate trays, check the temperature of each. All three solutions should be between 65° and 70° Fahrenheit. To cool a solution, place the jar in a large pan of cold water and stir the chemical until it reaches the recommended temperature. If the solution is too cool, use warm water in the pan.

Once you have poured the solutions into the trays and are ready to begin developing, blackout the darkroom. Take a square of film, place it in the developer and start timing. The correct amount of time is specified on the label of the developer you are using. If you're using a tri-chem-pak, the developing time is two minutes. Raise and lower the film several times.

24

When the time is up, remove the film from the developer and place it in the stop bath. It remains there for 15 to 20 seconds.

Next, place the film in the fixer. It stays in the fixer about 10 minutes, or until clear. When the 10 minutes have elapsed, you can turn on the lights.

Last, wash the film. Put the film in the tray containing the water and then put the tray in the sink and run water into it. The film should wash this way for about 30 minutes.

After the film is thoroughly washed, attach the film clip to one edge and hang it up to dry in a dust-free place. Don't forget to pour the chemicals back into their storage jars. (Figure 6.)

Figure 6.

When the negative is dry, examine it. If it is lacking in detail or, worse, if it is virtually transparent, it is *underexposed*. This condition results when insufficient light reaches the film. Retake the picture increasing the exposure time or, in the case of an adjustable camera, the size of the lens opening.

If the negative tends toward black or if it is virtually opaque, you have given the film too much light. You have *overexposed*. Decrease the exposure time or reduce the size of the lens opening when you reshoot.

When you have become experienced in developing, you will find that you can sometimes remedy the condition of underexposure or overexposure by the use of special chemicals. For example, by using an intensifying solution which increases printing density and negative contrast, underexposed negatives can be improved. A chemical with the reverse effect is available for overexposed negatives.

If you begin to develop rolls of film, you'll find it simpler to use a developing tank instead of following the tray method. A film developing tank simplifies the procedure because once the film is placed inside the tank and the cover put on, you can turn on the lights. With the tray method, of course, you must maintain a condition of darkness over the entire processing time, which can be as long as 20 minutes.

Besides the small, drum-shaped, plastic tank and its light-tight cover, the assembly includes a special spool upon which the film is wound and a spindle which you use to revolve the loaded spool once it's immersed in the chemicals. (Figure 7.)

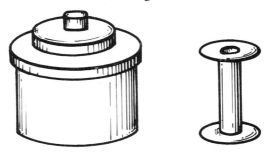

Figure 7.

You pour developer into the tank, and at the end of the developing time pour it out. You follow the same procedure with the stop bath and hypo. You also use the tank when it comes to washing the film.

Printing

Printing is the payoff, the culmination of all your efforts.

When making a print, you repeat the developing process. Light

26

is projected through the negative onto a sheet of light-sensitive paper. The blackest, most opaque areas of the negative hold back the light, allowing very little or perhaps no light at all to reach the paper. These are the whitest parts of the picture. Wherever the negative is thin, a great deal of light passes through, producing the darker or black portions of the photograph. After it is exposed to the light, the paper is developed and fixed.

In essence, what you are doing is making a negative of a negative, and the result is a positive—your picture.

The chemicals you require are developer, stop bath and fixer. You can use the same developer for printing as you did for developing film as long as it is "universal developer." If it isn't, you will have to purchase developer that is satisfactory for paper. The stop bath and fixer used for film can also be used for paper.

Printing paper comes in a wide range of types. For your first attempts at printing, ask for contact paper. Sometimes it is called "chloride paper" because silver chloride is used in making its light-sensitive emulsion.

Buy a size that matches the size of the negatives you are working with. Paper classed as "single weight," as opposed to "double weight," is usually the type used for making prints that are 5×7 inches in size or smaller.

You must also specify the type of surface texture you want. It can range from a coarse, almost clothlike texture, to a surface that is dull and lustreless, to a smooth, shiny, lustrous paper known as "glossy." Glossy paper is best for beginners.

Your dealer will also want to know what contrast grade of paper you want. The grade you choose depends upon the type of negatives you're using: Most beginners should specify contrast grades No. 2 or No. 3.

Photographic paper is sold in packages, a minimum of 25 sheets to a pack. Never open a packet except under safelight conditions.

You also need a printing frame. This consists of a heavy frame and a rectangular piece of glass that fits into it. The back of the frame is hinged and held firmly to the frame by a spring. What the printing frame does is to hold the negative and paper tightly in contact during the time of exposure. (Figure 8.)

Finally, you require a light source for making the exposure. Almost any lamp will do. Use an unshaded 100–watt frosted bulb.

Figure 8.

Arrange the four trays in a row on your table in the darkroom. From left to right, the developer goes into the first tray, stop bath in the second tray, fixer in the third tray, and water in the last tray. Check the temperature of the solutions before you put them in the trays.

Arrange the white light that is to make the exposure, your watch or timer and your printing frame on the worktable in the darkroom. Be sure you have sufficient working space so you won't be splashing chemicals into the area where you plan to do the printing.

Before you begin, check the glass of the printing frame to assure that it is perfectly clean, free of all fingerprints and dust particles. Also examine the negatives. Professional darkroom men use "anti-staticum" cloth on a camel's-hair brush to remove dust from negatives or the glass of the printing frame.

Put the negative in the printing frame. Be sure that the dull side of the negative faces up.

Turn off the white light; turn on the safelight. Now open the packet of printing paper. Break the seal and unwrap the package carefully because you'll want to rewrap all that is not used.

Be careful how you handle the paper, grasping it only at the edges. If you touch the paper in the center, you are likely to have a fingerprint in your final print.

Put the paper over the negative in the printing frame. The dull side of the negative should face the emulsion side—the slick, shiny side—of the paper. Close the lid and lock it.

Now make the exposure. Hold the printing frame, glass side up, about three feet from the 100–watt bulb. Turn the light on; keep it on for ten seconds, then turn it off.

Remove the exposed paper from the printing frame, again handling it by the edge. Slide it, shiny side up, into the developer. Use the stirring rod to shove the paper beneath the surface. (Figure 9.) If the solution does not cover the emulsion side of the paper quickly and uniformly, uneven development is likely to be the result. The print will look streaked.

Figure 9.

Rock the tray gently by tipping up one end and then the other. This keeps the solution flowing over the paper's surface.

Keep aware of the time. After approximately 60–90 seconds, take the paper out of the developer. Let the liquid drain off, then slide the paper face-down into the stop bath solution.

Rock the tray as before. The paper should remain in the stop-bath for about 15 seconds.

Next, fix the print. Remove it from the stop-bath and put it in the hypo. Tip the tray up and down. The print should remain in the fixer for 5-10 minutes. You can fix several prints at one time, but you must keep them separated. Prints that cling together are likely to be streaked.

After the print has been in the fixer for a minute or so, you can turn on the lights. Inspect your work. If the print is overexposed or underexposed, don't discard it. Leave it in the fixing tray so that you can compare it to your next attempt.

After fixing, transfer the print to the wash tray. Wash it in gently running water for at least 30 minutes. The water should be between 65° and 75° Fahrenheit.

Dry the print between a pair of blotters. Special photo blotters are sold for this purpose. Or you can place the print on a clean, lintless towel and cover it with a second towel.

Your first prints may be underexposed or overexposed but through trial and error you will quickly improve. Corrections should be made by varying the exposure time, that is, exposing the paper for a longer or shorter time.

Don't try to compensate in the developing stage. For example, if a print is still too light after 60 to 90 seconds in the developer, and you attempt to "force" it by letting it remain in the developer for an additional 2 or 3 minutes, the print that results is likely to lack in contrast, and will be fogged. A print that is yanked too soon from the developer will be flat and dull.

Once you become serious about darkroom work, you will probably want to switch from a simple printing frame to a contact printer, a more efficient piece of equipment. About the size of a small breadbox, the contact printer contains the printing light that produces the exposure. The negative is placed upon the sheet of frosted glass that serves as the top of the box. The cover is closed and the printing light switched on.

Whether you use a contact printer or a printing frame, the print you obtain is always the same size as the negative from which it is made. To get a print of increased size, you use an enlarger.

In enlarging, the negative is put into a holder which slips into the enlarger. An optically magnified image of the negative is projected onto an easel. Once the projection is in proper focus, a piece of printing paper is slipped beneath the metal arms of the easel. Then the paper is exposed. (Figure 10.)

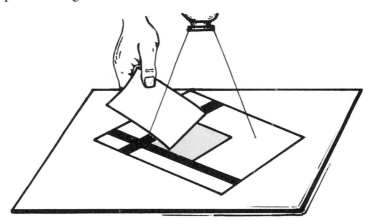

Figure 10.

The same procedure as in contact printing follows: developing the exposed paper, rinsing it in stop-bath, fixing it and then rinsing and drying it.

When you use an enlarger, you have a chance to act as an editor. You càn select for enlargement only those portions of the negative that make for a choice picture, a process known as *cropping*, and you can edit out defects or weaknesses which detract from the body of the picture.

If you find that these aspects of photography appeal to you, you might want to set up a permanent darkroom in your home. The basic requirement is a room that can be darkened for short periods of time.

You will also need facilities for storing your equipment, but even should you become a dedicated darkroom enthusiast, storage would not be a problem. You should not require any more space than that provided by a closet shelf or filing cabinet.

Of course, the most convenient way to have film developed and printed is to leave it at the corner drugstore or a camera shop, and then stop back in a day or two and pick up your prints.

But the problem here is that your work becomes caught up in a mass-production operation. You can't expect your prints to be of high quality.

When you do your own developing and printing, you exercise substantial control over the finished product. Your darkroom chemicals and tools also give you additional opportunity to use your creative skill.

That's not all. By having full knowledge of what happens in the darkroom, you become more sensitive to conditions of light and to composition when taking pictures. You become a more skilled photographer.

chapter 3

CAMERA CONTROLS

Cameras differ widely in design and construction but even the most sophisticated type when reduced to its simplest elements, is very similar to your coffee-can camera. It is simply a light-proof box which holds a variety of optical and mechanical parts.

The simplest cameras even resemble the coffee-can camera in the way they operate. You simply point and shoot. But more advanced models have several control systems that permit you to make pictures of technical excellence while at the same time expressing your thoughts and feelings about the subject.

All cameras have some type of viewfinding device to show you what you're getting on the film. Modern cameras boast optical viewfinding systems which involve mirrors and prisms. You use the viewfinder both in aiming the camera and composing the picture (a subject covered in Chapter 5).

The *lens* is the "eye" of the camera, an optical device that collects light rays from the subject and focuses them on the film. With the simplest camera the lens is merely a small glass disk or a circular piece of curved, transparent plastic. But with any advanced camera the lens consists of several pieces of optical glass mounted in a single unit.

With a sophisticated camera it's necessary to focus the lens. A knob control enables you to move the lens in and out, changing its distance from the film until you obtain the sharpest possible image of your subject. (With simple cameras the focus is fixed in such a way that objects beyond a few feet are in reasonable focus.)

Adjustable cameras also allow you to control *exposure*, the total amount of light admitted to the film. Exposure is a critical matter. If the film receives too much light, the resulting picture has a white, washed-out look (as you may have learned from the experiment in Chapter 2). This is overexposure. An underexposed photograph looks as if it had been taken in a closet at night.

An underexposed print (left) and an overexposed one. (George Sullivan)

There are two ways to control exposure. One is by controlling the brightness or intensity of the light the lens admits, and the second is by controlling the length of time the light is allowed to fall on the film. Think of a water faucet. The amount of water that flows from the faucet is controlled by how long you leave the faucet turned on. It is also controlled by how wide the faucet is opened; the water can trickle out or rush out.

With a camera, you increase exposure by letting brighter light into the camera or exposing for a longer period of time, or a combination of both. You reduce exposure by cutting the intensity of light and/or shortening the exposure time, or both.

Time Control; The Shutter—The *shutter* is a mechanical device inside the camera that opens and closes, allowing light to fall upon the film for a carefully measured amount of time. A push button or lever—the *shutter release*—enables you to trip the shutter. (Figure 11.)

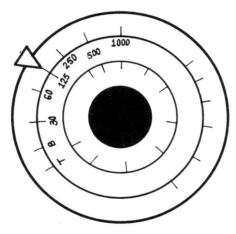

Figure 11.

The simplest cameras have a shutter that opens and closes at one fixed speed—about 1/50 of a second. Advanced cameras have shutter speeds ranging from 1/1000 of a second to one full second. The faster the shutter speed, the less time the lens is open, and the smaller the amount of light that strikes the film. The slower the shutter speed, the longer the lens is open, and the greater the amount of light admitted.

The range of shutter settings often runs like this: 1/1000, 1/500, 1/250, 1/60, 1/30, 1/15, 1/8, 1/4, 1/2 and one second. It's important to realize that when you move from one setting to the next fastest one—from 1/15 to 1/30, say—you are reducing the exposure by one half. When you go in the other direction, you are doubling the exposure. There is also a provision for time exposure (a "T" setting) or bulb exposure ("B" setting). These allow you to open the shutter for as long a time as you want.

Under normal conditions you are likely to shoot at 1/125 or 1/250 of a second. But it depends. For one thing, it depends on whether there is any movement in the scene.

You can use the shutter control system to "stop" a moving subject, that is, record the fact of its movement without any streaks or blurs. The shorter the shutter speed, the less time a moving object has to change its position while the shutter is open, so the less time the image transmitted to the film has to move. By shooting at 1/1000 of a second you can stop almost any kind of action. Of course, the reverse is true: with slow shutter speeds you get a high degree of movement, or blur.

When shooting action, there are several factors you have to consider. One is the direction of the action. If you stand in the middle of a road and watch a car that is coming toward you or going away, the car's speed seems a great deal less than if you are watching it from the same distance alongside the road. You have to be aware of this principle in determining shutter speeds. When motion relative to the camera is directly head-on, you can use a slower shutter speed than when you're attempting to record the same action at right angles to the camera.

Distance is a second factor that must be taken into consideration.

36

A 1/30 of a second (top), the boy's image is a blur; at 1/125 of a second (center), some bluriness remains, but at 1/500 of a second, all motion is frozen. (George Sullivan)

An automobile in the far distance may appear to be hardly moving, yet actually be traveling at 60 mph. But up close, a car traveling at that rate of speed will whiz by. The rule, then, is that the greater the distance between the subject and the camera, the less shutter speed you require. Extreme close-up action is almost impossible to stop. The chart on page 39 gives recommended shutter speeds for action photographs.

As mentioned, by using a shutter speed of 1/1000 of a second, you will be able to stop almost any type of action. But should this always be your goal? Probably not. The human eye does not freeze action, and so a small blur in your picture often adds a dash of excitement and makes it more realistic.

Photographers sometimes cope with action scenes by *panning*, which means swinging the camera horizontally with the moving subject. Suppose your target is an airplane taking off. Center the plane in your viewfinder. Then, turning your body from the waist, follow the subject in your viewfinder, click the shutter, and continue to follow the subject for a moment. The motion should be as smooth and unhurried as a tennis stroke. Press the shutter gently; don't jab at it. When panning is done properly, the subject will be recorded sharply and the background will be blurred, giving the feeling of movement to the picture.

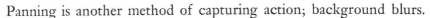

Panning is another method of capturing action; background blurs.

Shutter Speeds for Action Photographs

Subject	Distance between subject and camera	Direction of Motion		
		head on	at approx. 45° angle	at approx. 90° angle
children at play, pedestrians, parades, street scenes	10-15 feet	1/125	1/250	1/500
	25-50 feet	1/60	1/125	1/250
active sports (baseball, football, etc.) automobiles, trains, power boats	10-15 feet	1/500	1/500	1/1000
	25 feet	1/250	1/500	1/1000
	50 feet	1/125	1/250	1/500
speeding automobiles, aircraft, motorcycles, etc. at 60 mph and faster	10-15 feet	1/1000	1/1000	1/1000
	25 feet	1/500	1/1000	1/1000
	50 feet	1/250	1/500	1/1000

Controlling Light Intensity; the Iris Diaphragm—An ingenious device known as the *iris diaphragm* allows you to vary the size of the lens opening, thus regulating the brightness of the light that enters the camera. Named after the iris of the human eye, the iris diaphragm consists of thin leaves of metal arranged to overlap in such a way that they form a circular opening of variable size.

The larger the lens opening—or *aperture*, as it is called—the greater the intensity of the light that enters. A small aperture means less brightness. (Figure 12.)

f/16   f/11   f/8   f/5.6

Figure 12.

The aperture adjustment is usually located on or near the lens mount. It is calibrated with a series of *f* numbers or *stops*. (The *f* preceding a number signifies a relationship between the lens opening and its focal length.) The full range of *f* stops includes the following: *f*/1, *f*/1.4, *f*/2, *f*/2.8, *f*/4, *f*/5.6, *f*/11, *f*/16, *f*/22, *f*/32, and *f*/64. (Figure 13.)

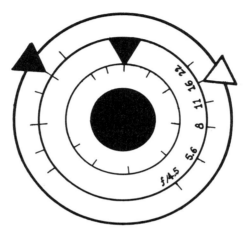

Figure 13.

The range of stops is not the same for every lens. The lens that comes with your camera is likely to be a "fast" lens, with the range of stops beginning as low as *f*/1.4, while a telescopic lens might begin with *f*/4.

The critical point to remember concerning aperture is that the smaller the *f* number, the larger the lens opening, and the larger the number the smaller the opening. (Smaller numbers such as *f*/2 and *f*/2.8 represent larger openings than, say, *f*/11 or *f*/16 because the *f* numbers are denominators of fractions. Just remember that 1/2 is larger than 1/4, and so forth.) So whenever you move to a smaller *f* number, you are opening the diaphragm and increasing the brightness of light admitted to the film, and vice versa.

There is a close relationship between the *f*-numbers and the amount of light admitted. Opening up one full stop *doubles* the intensity of light admitted to the film. Closing down one full stop *cuts the intensity of light in half.*

The principle is easy to understand if you square the numbers involved. For example, suppose you want to find out how much more light is admitted by a setting of *f*/2 than at *f*/4. Square the numbers. You get 4 and 16 respectively. Since 16 is four times as much as 4, it means that your *f*/2 setting gives you four times as much brightness as the *f*/4 setting.

With most of today's cameras, it's not necessary to do such figuring. The *f* numbers used are arranged in such a way that moving one full stop to a lower *f* number doubles the brightness, while moving one full stop toward a higher *f* number cuts it in half.

Getting the Right Exposure — As explained above, there are two independent systems for controlling exposure: the shutter controls time; the aperture controls intensity. And the two work in a carefully balanced relationship.

For example, suppose you are taking a picture of a sailboat as it comes toward you. You are using a shutter speed of 1/125 of a second to stop the action, and the condition of light is such that you're using an aperture setting of *f*/8.

Suddenly the sailboat shifts direction and starts moving at right angles to you. You immediately switch to a faster shutter speed to stop the motion, to 1/250 of a second. But since you have cut the duration of the exposure in half, you are almost certain to produce an underexposed picture. So you must compensate by opening the aperture another stop. You must switch from *f*/8 to *f*/5.6. When you shoot at 1/250 and *f*/5.6, you get exactly the same exposure as when your settings were 1/125 and *f*/8. The same holds true if you moved the settings in the other direction—to 1/60 and *f*/11.

The number of combinations which will produce a given

exposure is limited only by the number of settings of the camera. You don't have to memorize all the combinations, but you must be aware of the fundamental relationship between shutter speed and lens aperture. If you close down the aperture by one stop, you must go to the next slowest speed setting. If you open the aperture by two stops, you need to increase your shutter speed two notches.

All of this may be time-consuming at first. But if you understand the basic principles involved, it will soon become a simple matter and you'll be making the necessary adjustments quickly and mechanically.

Depth of Field — Besides the effect it has on the intensity of light transmitted to the film, lens aperture also affects the sharpness of the image. It affects what is known as *depth of field*, the area in which objects appear sharp, both behind and in front of the point on which you have focused. Succinctly, depth of field is your zone of focus.

The rule to remember is this: Decrease the size of the aperture and you increase depth of field; increase aperture and you decrease depth of field. Suppose you're taking pictures of a parade. The high school band comes marching by and you want each row of bandsmen to appear sharp and distinct. To achieve this, you should "stop down the lens"—go to a smaller aperture, maybe from $f/11$ to $f/16$. (This means you'll have to compensate, of course, by slowing the shutter speed a notch.)

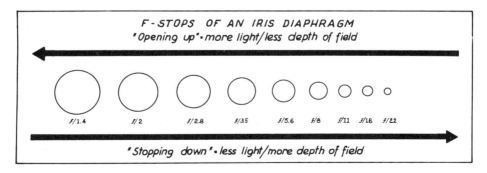

Figure 14.

There will be other times when total sharpness is detrimental to your picture. If you are taking pictures of a child at play, you might feel it's distracting to have nearby children in sharp focus. To make them indistinct, you would use a large aperture, perhaps going from *f*/5.6 to *f*/4 (and compensating by using a faster shutter speed).

Keep in mind that depth of field gets progressively less as you focus on closer and closer objects. This means that when you're taking a close-up, you have to be extra careful in focusing, even if the aperture you're using is a small one.

Most modern cameras have a depth-of-field scale engraved on the lens mount or at the focusing control. This scale reports how

Cards in photo at left are indistinct, but decreasing the size of the aperture serves to increase the depth of field, bringing them into sharp focus. (Honeywell Inc., Photographic Products Division)

much depth of field you're getting with the combination of aperture and focusing distance you happen to be using. Consult your camera's instruction manual.

With knowledge of the depth-of-field principle, you can preset your camera to enable you to shoot quickly without stopping to focus. Suppose you're taking pictures at a tennis match from a position of 30 or 40 feet away from the court. The easiest way to get a picture of one of the players executing a shot is to check your depth-of-field scale to determine what the near and far limits of sharp focus will be. When the player enters the zone, shoot.

Summing Up — From this chapter, you should derive an understanding of these three camera control systems:

• the focus control, which enables you to get a sharp image of your subject.

• the shutter, which controls the amount of time that light is focused on the film.

• the aperture control system, which regulates the intensity of light.

Shutter speed and lens aperture control exposure. To arrive at a correct exposure, first determine whether you want to stop action or control depth of field.

If stopping the action is your goal, first select the shutter speed and then choose the corresponding lens aperture—an *f* stop—that will give you correct exposure.

On the other hand, if controlling depth of field is your aim, first select the lens aperture setting you require and then set the shutter speed.

Last, remember that anytime you switch to a faster shutter speed, you must also open the lens aperture. Slow the shutter speed, and you must close down the lens. And, of course, the reverse is true; open or close the lens aperture and you must make the requisite changes in shutter speed.

chapter **4**

CHOOSING a CAMERA, FILM and ACCESSORIES

Any person new to the world of photography who has ever visited a large supply shop to buy a camera has to be bewildered by the dazzling array of merchandise available. There may be as many as a thousand cameras on display, and they vary widely in style and size, and in price they range from a few dollars to a thousand dollars and more.

Yet if you pursue your choice in a logical manner, it will not be difficult to make a sound decision. First of all, you want to obtain a camera that puts you in control; otherwise, you will never be able to make pictures which boast a professional quality. This element of control is derived from a fully adjustable camera, one that allows you to focus, to adjust the lens aperture and control shutter speeds, topics discussed in the previous chapter.

Cameras with adjustable control systems begin at about $50. You can save money by shopping carefully. Study the catalogs published by major equipment manufacturers that describe their cameras and give "list prices." But keep in mind that these prices are mere guidelines. Seldom will a dealer expect you to pay the list price for anything, a fact that is especially true if you shop in a metropolitan area. However, each store has a different discount structure. That's

45

why you should visit several camera stores and price and compare before you make your decision.

Be sure you are accompanied by a photographer or a person who is knowledgeable about cameras, someone to help you bargain. If you know somebody who has a working relationship with a camera store, ask him to help you. People who know salesmen usually get better deals than people who don't.

A salesperson may ask you whether you are interested in buying a second hand camera, and state a price that is substantially below that of a new camera of the same type. Be wary. As a general rule, it is not wise to buy a used camera. "You're just taking on someone else's problems," says one expert in the field.

Camera Types

Any camera can be classified by two main features: (1) the type of film it uses, and (2) the kind of viewfinding system it has.

When it comes to film, a camera may use familiar roll film in any one of a number of sizes, or sheet film, in the case of a "big" camera, the kind used by professional studio photographers. Roll film includes the popular 120 (12 2¼×2¼-inch negatives to a roll) or 220 (24 negatives of this size per roll), and 127 and 620, the type used in box cameras. (Figure 15.)

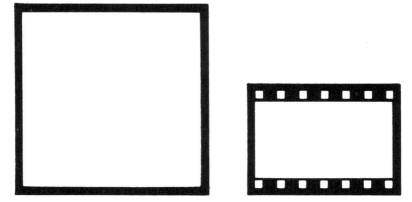

Figure 15.

A 35 mm cassette. (George Sullivan)

There is also 35 mm film, so called because it is 35 millimeters in width. A metal cartridge or "cassette," of 35 mm film gives 20 or 36 exposures, each one a bit larger than a postage stamp.

Viewfinding systems vary from an open wire frame, the most primitive type, to complex optical systems involving carefully mounted mirrors and prisms. With some viewfinding systems, you hold the camera to your eye. With others, the camera is held at waist level.

One other point before discussing camera types in detail. Many of today's cameras are "automatic" in that they have a built-in electric eye which measures light reflected from the subject and automatically sets the exposure. If the camera you decide upon has this feature, be sure it also allows you to bypass the automatic control and set the shutter speed and lens aperture manually. In other words, your camera should always allow you to exercise creative freedom.

Box Cameras — The box camera is the simplest to operate and least expensive of all camera types. You load the film, aim, and snap. Everything more than five or six feet away will be in focus.

Box cameras usually have viewfinder windows to aid in aiming. The picture in the window is often comparable in size to the actual negative made by the camera.

The elementary nature of the box camera suggests its disadvantages. The simple lens prevents taking sharp pictures under certain conditions. The fixed or, at least, limited shutter speeds and aperture settings make it difficult to get pictures in poor light (without resorting

The box camera. (Eastman Kodak Company)

to flash). A romping child, a running horse—almost any type of fast motion—is a problem for the box camera.

The box camera is ideal for snapshot photography, for taking pictures of your friends at the beach or at a relative's birthday party. But such cameras present serious limitations for anyone with a serious interest in photography. The box camera is not adequate as a training tool, either. It teaches little about such vital elements as exposure and focus.

Polaroid Cameras — "Instant photography" is what you get with the Polaroid camera. Seconds after you have snapped the shutter you have a permanent black and white print. The negative is developed inside the camera, then used to expose a positive print, which is then itself developed. Such magic would have astounded photographers of a generation ago.

The Polaroid firm improves the camera constantly, bringing out new and different models and ingenious accessory items. Surely

This is Polaroid's "Color Pack" Camera. (Polaroid Corporation)

the greatest advance since the Polaroid was first announced was the introduction of Polacolor film, which permits you to get a finished color print 50 seconds after you have taken the picture. Built-in exposure meters and transistorized shutters are other recent advances. Since the Polaroid system does not produce a negative which can be used to make additional prints, the company markets a print copier.

No one denies that Polaroid cameras have serious limitations when it comes to distinguished photography. Yet Polaroids are extremely popular and growing in popularity all the time, and this is understandable.

35 mm Rangefinder — The viewing system here is a step up the ladder from the optical viewfinder common to box cameras and Polaroids. While it does utilize an optical viewfinder, it combines it with a focusing device known as a rangefinder. This system enables you to get a sharp, clear focus, no matter the condition of light.

A 35 mm rangefinder camera. (Bell & Howell, Consumer Products Group)

Twin-Lens Reflex — As the name suggests, the twin-lens reflex camera has two lenses, one above the other. The top lens, unlike a conventional lens, has no shutter or iris diaphragm. It is used for view-finding and focusing. The bottom lens takes the picture.

The lenses are mounted on the same plane, which means that when you revolve the knob to sharpen focus, you are also focusing the taking lens. The image of the subject is reflected by means of a mirror system onto a hooded square of groundglass at the top of the camera.

The bulk of twin-lens reflex cameras use 120 or 220 film. Since film of this type produces negatives that are 2¼ × 2¼ inches in size, the prints that result are large enough for viewing without enlarging.

A twin-lens reflex camera. (Yashica)

If you do wish to enlarge, the results can be exceptional because of the negative size. The film size presents something of a problem with color photography, however, for you require a projector of larger-than-normal size to screen your transparencies.

Besides the large viewing area which permits you to see exactly what will be recorded on the negative, the twin-lens reflex has many other advantages. It is rugged and compact. It produces photos of first-rate quality and is also unrivaled as an educational tool, offering easy-to-understand, simple-to-operate, lens opening and shutter speed systems.

The twin-lens reflex is a standard professional camera. The renowned Rollieflex is the classic example of cameras of this type, but all companies market them.

One of the drawbacks of the twin-lens reflex is that most models do not permit you to interchange lenses (see below). You have to rely on the lens that is in the camera for every type of situation; however, an ever-increasing number of manufacturers are beginning to offer the interchangeability feature.

Single Lens Reflex — More than a few experts declare that the 35 mm single-lens reflex camera is what triggered the boom in photography in recent years. While this statement may be debated, it is a fact that it is the most wanted, if not the most used, of all camera types.

It's not difficult to understand why. The single-lens reflex, like the twin-lens type, uses a mirror to reflect to the photographer's eye the image being seen by the camera lens. But the viewing lens and taking lens are one and the same.

The image is transmitted to the view-finder by means of a clever mirror system. When you trip the shutter to make the exposure, you also, by the same finger pressure, spring a release that swings the mirror out of the way, thus allowing the image to be projected on the film.

52

A 35 mm single-lens reflex camera. (Honeywell Inc., Photographic Products Group)

This superb viewing system has been married to cameras of many types, including those that take pictures of 2¼×2¼ inches in size, but the single lens reflex concept has found its greatest popularity in combination with cameras using 35 mm film. Such cameras are small in size and light in weight. Indeed, sometimes they are classified as miniature cameras.

As a general rule, 35 mm single-lens reflex cameras offer lens aperture and shutter speed control systems that are more sophisticated than those contained in twin-lens reflex models. Virtually all 35 mm single-lens reflex cameras feature the principle of interchangeable lenses and have the ability to use a wide range of accessory items.

53

Most cameras of this type being purchased are of Japanese manufacture, which has been the case since the late 1940's. Nikon, Canon, Asahi (Pentax) and Minolta are among the leaders in the field.

Should a beginner use a camera of this type? Indeed. The most serious problem he will face is likely to be one of cost. The single lens reflex camera is priced at four to six times what the twin-lens reflex costs.

Ultraminiature Cameras — Its light weight and compactness—some models can be concealed in the palm of the hand—make the ultraminiature camera popular with those who want to take photographs without attracting attention. In fact, cameras of this type are sometimes promoted as "spy cameras." They offer many features of cameras of conventional size, nevertheless.

Some models use special 16 mm film or smaller, which requires special processing and adds to the expense. But there are models now available which utilize 35 mm frames. You thus get 72 pictures to the casette. Such cameras are not quite so tiny as the usual ultraminiature, but they're compact enough to carry unnoticed in one's jacket pocket.

An ultraminiature camera.
(Minox)

54

View Cameras — The view camera is standard equipment for the professional studio photographer. It features a large pane of groundglass which fits over the back of the camera and is used for viewing and focusing.

The view camera does everything and has everything. It takes a wide range of lenses and just about any accessory item you can name. Using sheet film it provides the largest negatives, 4×5, 5×7 or 8×10 in size. The front of the camera, including the lens mount, can be swung or tilted in any direction to correct for distortion.

Such a camera, however, isn't practical for the young amateur. It's expensive; it's heavy and bulky. And the large-size film it requires adds to the expense.

The view camera is standard equipment among professionals. (Wagner International Photos Inc.)

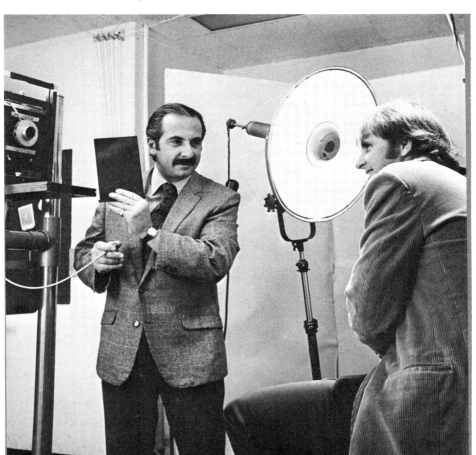

Film

In choosing black and white film your primary consideration should be the matter of emulsion speed or, simply, speed. This refers to the film's sensitivity to light. Films with the greatest degree of sensitivity require little exposure, and thus you can use them to take pictures in dim light.

Film is rated as to its speed by the American Standards Association (the ASA Rating) and, in Europe, by the Deutsche Industrie Norm (the DIN Rating). Both ASA and DIN numbers are given on the information sheet packed with each film roll. The higher the rating, the greater the speed. Kodak's all purpose Verichrome film has an ASA rating of 125, while the company's high speed Tri-X film has a 400 rating.

A high speed film gives you greater freedom because you never have to pass up taking a picture because of the absence of light. It also enables you to use the higher shutter speeds necessary in capturing action photographs. But there's a disadvantage—graininess.

The silver grains that go to form a photograph are larger in the faster films. When the negative is developed and enlarged to eight or nine times its original size, it may begin to show a "salt-and-pepper" effect in the middle tone areas. To some extent, this graininess can be overcome by specifying fine grain development when you bring the film to the photo finisher.

The matter of grain is no problem if you are using a camera that produces a negative that is 2¼×2¼ inches in size. It is only with the 35 mm enlargements that graininess may manifest itself.

Up until recent years, black and white film was classified as orthochromatic or panchromatic. Orthochromatic film is blind to red, while panchromatic is sensitive to all colors of the spectrum. You may encounter these terms when reading a photography handbook. Don't be concerned about the problem, however, because virtually all film has "pan" sensitivity today.

Get into the habit of reading the information sheet each time you open a package of film. Don't be concerned with the manufacturer's brand names, such as Verichrome, Pantomatic or whatever. The film's speed rating is what's important.

Once you've found a film with a speed that gives you good results consistently, stay with it. This is practice that professionals follow.

Color Film — One basic difference between black and white film and color is that the latter has three emulsions, each of which is sensitive to a different color. This fact makes it necessary that you exercise greater care when taking color pictures.

Imagine a strip of color film as a three-decker sandwich, each layer about 3/1000 of an inch thick. The top layer is an emulsion sensitive only to blue. Beneath is an emulsion which reacts only to green. The third layer is sensitive only to red. The film base is similar as that on black and white film, and has an anti-halation backing that prevents the light rays from scattering and blurring the image.

The multi-layer construction of color film results in film speeds that are much lower than those of black and white film. Some of the newer color films are rated at ASA 200, but this is an exception. The popular Kodacolor-X Film, for example, has a rating of ASA 80. What this means is that your exposure range is somewhat limited when you use color.

When buying color film, you have to choose between two different types—reversal or negative. The reversal type is developed first as a negative, then by re-exposing and redeveloping is reversed to produce a positive image. What results is a color *transparency*, which is viewed by means of a slide projector.

The negative type of color film registers the opposite of colors being photographed, then during processing is transferred to the true color value. What you get are color prints.

Film manufacturers use such a variety of trade names in describing their color film that it is not difficult to become confused. But you will be able to keep them straight if you bear in mind that color film names ending in "chrome"—Ekta*chrome*, Koda*chrome*, Agfa*chrome*, etc.—produce transparencies. Names ending in "color—Koda*color*, for example—give color prints.

Lenses

When you purchase an advanced camera, either a twin-lens reflex or a 35 mm model, it will be equipped with a standard lens, a workhorse lens, one that can be used to make a wide variety of photographs. Later, when your work begins to become more specialized, you may want to start acquiring additional lenses.

Lenses are classified by their *speed* and *focal length*. Speed refers to the light-transmitting ability of a lens. Generally speaking, a "fast" lens transmits more light to the film than a "slow" lens. This doesn't mean that the fast lens takes better pictures. In fact, it may produce pictures that are not as sharp as some slow lenses.

Lens speed is measured in terms of the size of the largest possible aperture, and this is expressed by an *f*-number, such as *f*/1.4 or *f*/2 or *f*/4. The smaller the *f*-number, the faster the lens.

Focal length is likely to be of greater importance to you than speed, for it determines how much or how little of a scene will be included in the picture area taken from a given distance. By dictionary definition, focal length is the distance from the lens to the film when the camera is focused on the "infinity" mark.

A lens with a shorter than average focal length will record a scene that is broader than a normal lens would from the same camera positon. It takes a wide angle view, a panoramic view. A lens with a longer than normal focal length takes a reduced portion of the scene but, like a telescope, gives a king-sized image of whatever it focuses on.

58

A sample of lenses to be used with a 35 mm camera. (Bell & Howell, Consumer Products Group)

Focal length is measured in millimeters, and lenses range in size from about 21 mm to 1000 mm. It is likely that your camera came equipped with a lens of from between 50 mm-80 mm.

You might want to purchase a wide-angle lens if much of your work is done in limited space and you are unable to get a great distance from what you are photographing. A lens of, say, 24 mm

59

or 28 mm would allow you to take a picture of a room interior or a building on a narrow street. Although they contain the greatest number of elements, sometimes as many as ten or more, wide angle lenses are the most compact of all.

Telephoto lenses range in size from 200 mm to 1000 mm, but it is not likely you will ever require a lens greater than 400 mm. This type enables you to photograph a football player from the stands and get almost a close-up effect.

The (28 mm) wide angle lenses at the right contain many more elements than the (300 mm) telephoto lens. (Minolta Corporation)

Telephoto lenses have an extremely narrow angle of view. With a 400 mm lens, it's a mere 6°. A 24 mm lens offers an 84° angle of view.

60

Opposite: Lenses of different sizes increase your versatility. (Honeywell Inc.)

Telephoto lenses are sometimes used for portrait pictures. A 200 mm lens, for example, allows you to take a person's picture unobtrusively because you're a good distance away.

When you visit an equipment shop to purchase a lens, be certain to take along your camera. Attach the lens to the camera to be sure the fit is perfect, not the least bit too loose or tight.

Accessory Items

Equipment manufacturers have taxed their imaginations to the fullest in developing accessories, and have developed gadgets and gimmicks in an infinite array. It is no wonder that the "gadget happy" photographer is not at all uncommon. Beware of the tendency to load up on equipment you will seldom use. Acquire accessories gradually, and only after you've become thoroughly proficient with your camera and are seeking to extend your capability. The paragraphs that follow will serve to guide you.

Lens Shade — This is one of the most practical purchases you can make. The lens shade (or hood) shields the lens from direct light rays that cause glare and reduce contrast. There's a size to fit every lens. A lens shade costs about $2. Use it for indoor or outdoor photography.

Lens shades and covers. (George Sullivan)

Exposure Meter — Used correctly, the exposure meter almost guarantees perfectly exposed pictures. Experts agree there are few accessories more useful. It is a meter in the true sense. A light-sensitive cell causes a needle to move on a scale to indicate how much light there is. A circular dial then translates the reading into an *f* number. Even if your camera has a built-in meter, you should consider owning one of these. They cost $15 and up.

An exposure meter.
(Minolta Corporation)

A filter. (Eastman Kodak Company)

Filters — Correct use of the proper filter can turn an ordinary black and white photo into a dramatic picture. A filter is simply a disk of colored glass that fixes to the front of the lens. It screens out certain rays of light and emphasizes others.

There are filters of dozens of different colors and intensities of color. The general rule to remember is this: A filter tends to lighten objects of the same color and darken those of complementary colors.

The most frequently used filter is light yellow. It lightens the yellowishness of flesh tones and, when used on a bright and sunny day, it darkens the blue sky, thus accentuating cloud whiteness.

A medium red filter dramatically darkens the sky. A light green filter is often used for outdoor portrait work because it helps retain normal flesh tones while darkening the sky.

Filters absorb some of the light that would normally strike the film; to compensate, an increase of one full stop in exposure is required in most cases. Filters are priced from $1.00.

Tripods — It's just about impossible to hand-hold a camera and get sharp pictures at slow speeds, 1/50 of a second or slower. The solution is a tripod. Get a sturdy, lightweight model with telescoping legs and a tilt-top head which allows you to move the camera in any direction. Some have crank-operated elevating devices that allow you to raise and lower the camera without adjusting the legs. Tripods cost $15-$25.

It's likely that you'll also want to purchase a gadget bag to hold your extra lenses, filters, etc. Get one of ample size and of rugged construction.

What else you need depends on what kind of photography you're going to be doing and how much of it. Go slowly—buy only what you really need and will use.

A tripod enables you to get sharp pictures at slow speeds. Photographer is using a cable release. (Wagner International Photos Inc.)

chapter **5**

USING YOUR CAMERA

Once you've purchased a camera, get to know it thoroughly. Study the camera together with the instruction manual that accompanies it. Know the function of every knob and button. Know what every setting and marking means.

Pay particular attention to the instructions concerning the loading of film. Set aside a roll of film for practice purposes and load it over and over—until you can do it automatically.

Always make certain that the emulsion side of the film faces the lens. With standard roll film, the emulsion side is the black side of the paper leader. With 35 mm film, it is the cream-colored side.

Be sure the spool or film cassette is firmly seated before you insert the leader into the slot of the take-up spool. Turn the advance mechanism slowly at first, until you determine that the film is securely fastened and running smoothly. Never force anything. If something doesn't move or turn easily, there is a reason. Check what you've done. Consult the instruction booklet.

How to Hold a Camera — Precisely how you hold your camera depends on its type and where the controls are located. It's also a matter of personal preference, for there is no one "right" way of holding. There are, however, certain suggestions you should follow.

The first rule is to hold the camera securely. Use both hands. Don't merely squeeze it with the tips of your fingers, but cradle it in both palms.

Keep your elbows tucked close to your body, but not so tightly as to cause muscle tension. Be relaxed; be comfortable. Be sure you can handle the controls with facility.

As you focus, keep your knees slightly bent, your legs apart a bit, and one foot just ahead of the other. Distribute your weight evenly on both feet. This stance gives you maximum steadiness.

Practice using the shutter release. Learn to press it gently. It's a smooth, squeezing action, not a poke or a jab.

If you shoot many pictures at slow shutter speeds, learn breath control to help assure camera steadiness. As you get ready to trip the shutter, inhale; then let out part of the breath, click the shutter, then exhale the rest of the way.

If you use a twin-lens reflex camera, hold it slightly above waist level, adjusting the neck strap so that it supports the camera. Work the focus control with your left hand, the shutter with your right.

When using the magnifier for critical focusing, bring the camera close to your eye. Loop your thumbs through the neckstrap to make the strap taut.

If you have a 35mm camera, use your right hand to support it, keeping your forefinger free to operate the shutter release. Use your left hand to press the camera against your face.

As you focus, be sure you have a solid stance. (George Sullivan)

Above: Hold the twin-lens reflex camera at about waist level. Above, right: This is how to make taut the neckstrap when using the magnifier. (George Sullivan)

Right: Hold the 35 mm camera firmly with both hands; keep your elbows in. (George Sullivan)

Focusing Control — Faulty focusing, which results in a picture that tends toward fuzziness, is a common failing among beginners.

The closer you are to your subject, the more careful you must be. In close-up photography, even a slight degree of error can cause the subject to be substantially out of focus.

Adjustable cameras offer a scale, marked in feet and inches, to help you focus. You first estimate the distance from your camera to the subject, then set the focusing scale accordingly. But this system has the obvious failing that it is not always possible to estimate the distance accurately. So cameras have a second and more reliable focusing system, either a groundglass or a rangefinder. (Figure 16.)

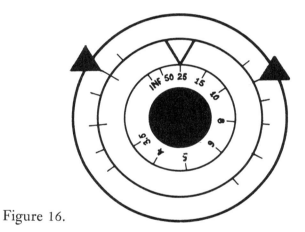

Figure 16.

With the former, common to the twin-lens reflex camera, you watch the image on the groundglass and continue adjusting the focus control knob until the image becomes sharp. The easiest way to achieve this sharpness is to move the focus control back and forth several times through the point of sharpest focus. Gradually reduce the back-and-forth movement until you reach a point where even the slightest movement of the focusing control causes image detail to become fuzzy. This is your point of sharpest focus.

68

Most 35 mm cameras offer rangefinder focusing. When you look through the viewfinder, you see small concentric circles of brightness within the viewing area. You rotate the focusing knob until one circle covers the other, which brings the image into sharp focus.

If your subject is moving, it may be almost impossible to keep it in focus. Here's what to do: Focus on a point over which the object will pass. When the subject reaches the focusing target, take the picture.

It takes a great deal of practice—months of it—to learn how to focus quickly and accurately. Practice focusing under different conditions of light and upon objects both near and far away. There are few aspects of photography as important as this.

Errors and How to Avoid Them — Even the most experienced professionals make mistakes occasionally and a poor, perhaps unusable, picture is the result. You can keep errors to minimum if you make up your mind not to rush things. Never make a picture simply by aiming the camera and clicking the shutter. Think. Plan. Take your time.

The most frequent slip-ups, aside from carlessness in focusing, have to do with exposure. If you often switch from film of one ASA rating to another, get in the habit of checking the film-speed setting before you use the camera.

Exposure errors are also caused by going from a brightly-lighted subject to a dimly-lit one—without changing the aperture or shutter speed. Be sure to check your exposure settings frequently.

Watch out for *parallax*, which is the difference between what you see in your viewfinder and what is to appear on the film. This problem is common to some twin-lens reflex cameras, models in which the top lens, the finding lens, has not been "corrected." It is on a different level from the taking lens, so what you see through the viewfinder is not exactly what the lens sees.

The problem of parallax becomes more obvious in closeups.

Watch out for parallax error (left). Tilt the camera upward slightly to overcome the problem (right).

The top of the subject may be cutoff. In this type of situation, tilting the camera upward slightly will correct for parallax.

Remember, it's a *slight* tilt. Too much tilting can result in a distorted picture. This frequently occurs when a tall building is the subject. In order to get the entire building in the viewfinder, the photographer tilts the camera sharply. The result is that the building looks as if it is falling away, falling backward.

70

Opposite: Tilting a camera too much can give a building a falling-backward look. (George Sullivan)

If your pictures have a soft, slightly fuzzy look, it may be because you're moving the camera during exposure. You can overcome this by practicing until you develop a firm grip on your camera. Squeeze the shutter release; don't jab at it.

Hold the camera perfectly still when you shoot or you're likely to get this type of fuzziness. (George Sullivan)

72

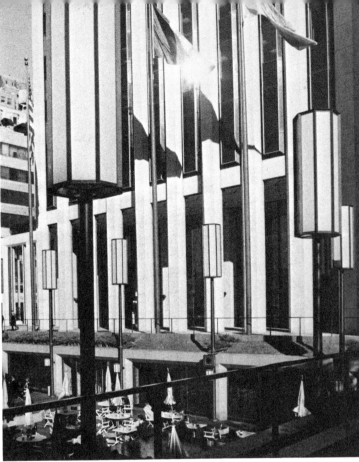

Dark streak in this picture was caused by a strap over the lens. (Left.) Photo "hot spot" comes from reflecting sun's rays. (Right.) (George Sullivan)

If the fuzziness is limited to a small portion of the picture, it's likely that the camera strap or one of your fingers got in front of the lens as you were shooting. If your subject is fuzzy but the rest of the picture is sharp and clear, your shutter speed wasn't fast enough to stop the action.

Watch out for bright sunlight, not only direct rays but also reflected rays from glass or bright surfaces. Rays from the sun that enter your lens will give a picture a "hot spot."

Use a rubber syringe to blow dust from the lens and other parts of the camera. (George Sullivan)

Camera Care — Like any precision instrument, your camera needs care and maintenance. While there are only a few chores you have to perform, each one is important.

Dust is your camera's worst enemy. Rid the camera of dust by blowing it away with a long-tipped rubber syringe. Get into every corner and crevice.

Use the syringe to clean the viewfinder and lens, too. Or you can gently blow on the lens and then brush it with a clean sable or camel's-hair brush. These are sold in camera shops.

Never try to clean a lens with a cloth. It may scratch the lens. Facial tissue or even silicone eyeglass tissue can cause damage to the extremely thin reflection coating common to modern lenses. Use special paper sold in camera shops.

Touching the lens can also be harmful. Perspiration from your fingers acts like an acid and in time will actually etch its way into the lens surface.

Protect your camera from extremes of temperature and conditions of high humidity. If the camera should happen to get wet,

74

dry it off immediately. Obtain a cabinet or locker in which you can store the camera. If you do not have a case for it, keep it in a plastic bag.

Don't leave the shutter cocked when storing the camera. Prolonged tension serves to weaken the spring mechanism.

Never attempt to make camera repairs yourself. When service is needed, take the camera to a photo shop, to the store where you purchased it, if possible, or to a franchised representative of the manufacturer. As a last resort, write to the manufacturer for advice about where the camera can be sent for service.

Improving Your Work — When you have film developed, order an 8×10-inch contact proof sheet for each roll of film. Study each proof sheet with a critical eye.

Keep proofs in handy files. A good system is to punch holes in the sheets and place them in a three-ring binder. Store the negatives in a small box, like a shoe box. Establish a system of numbers or letters for marking and identifying the proof sheets and the related glassine envelopes containing the negatives.

From time to time, look through the accumulated proof sheets to determine areas in which you are showing improvement and which require attention.

Studying your proof sheets will help you determine your strong and weak points. (George Sullivan)

Keep a file of the work of other photographers, clipping distinctive photos from newspapers and magazines. Photography magazines are another good source. Such files help to stimulate your imagination and will do much to improve your work.

Get into the habit of reading the photography section of your newspaper. Visit photographic exhibits. Study books containing the work of noted photographers, many of which are certain to be available at your local library.

There is, however, no substitute for taking photographs. You should have almost a formal schedule, taking pictures on a once- or twice-a-week basis. Photography, unlike stamp collecting or playing tennis, can be practiced almost anytime—on your way to school or the store, whether you're alone or with friends, indoors or outdoors.

Many photographers establish a personal picture-taking project, directing their efforts toward a particular subject. It can be people or pets, sports or architecture—anything. The important thing is to use your camera frequently. It's the only way to sharpen your skills.

chapter **6**

COMPOSITION

What makes a picture look "right"? What gives it meaning? Often it is good composition.

Composition refers to the selection and arrangement of the elements of a picture in a unified and pleasing manner. These elements are the various shapes, lines and tonal qualities of the subject. The ability to organize these with a sense of harmony and proportion is necessary to good photography.

Composition is a very personal matter. Any person, without even the slightest training, can look at a picture and, if there is an essential conflict of the picture's elements, know that the composition is not right. The picture is disturbing in some way. While people have this natural ability, there are certain basic principles of composition that can be taught. That's the purpose of this section.

Center of Interest — When you prepare to take a picture, your first thought should be to establish a center of interest, a focal point for everything the scene will contain. This doesn't mean that the subject has to be at the physical center of the photograph. What it does mean is that it should dominate the scene, if not physically then emotionally or psychologically.

And it doesn't mean that the subject has to be one object or

77

even a handful. An infinite number can be involved. Center of interest implies that elements contained in the picture tell a story. But only *one* story.

Compose the picture on your viewfinder, studying the entire scene from top to bottom, then from side to side. Be sure that the center of interest is clearly defined, that it stands out clearly from the background.

Ask yourself whether there are any distracting or irrelevant

Make your picture tell a story. (George Sullivan)

details in the picture. Check to see that no ruinous effects are to appear, such as a tree trunk or pole apparently growing out of a person's head.

Don't hesitate to move in close as you compose. In this way you limit the picture area, and meaningless details are eliminated. There is little or no wasted space. Novice photographers—many amateurs, in fact—have a reluctance to "get in tight." Yet the close-up photo has enormous impact. Look at the pictures in your local newspaper or a news magazine. The chances are good that most were taken up close.

Don't hesitate to get in close.
(George Sullivan)

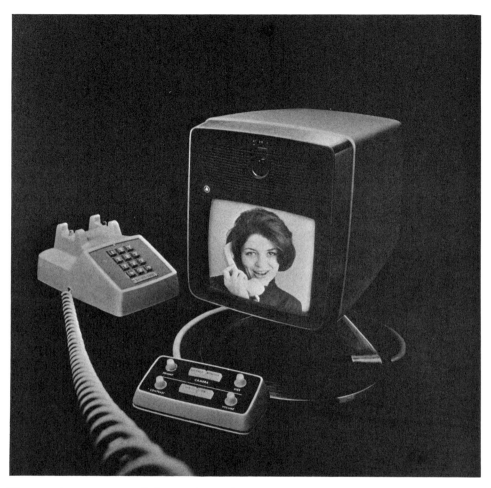

Clever arrangement of the various elements makes this a distinctive picture. (AT&T)

Arrangement and Balance — The various elements that make up a composition should work together to create a single impression. If they don't, the person viewing the picture will get a confused message.

80

The general rule is to arrange the various elements so that the eye moves in a logical sequence from one to another. If you are photographing two objects of similar size and they are at equal distance from the camera, and you retain their size relationship when you take the picture, you will get a balanced picture, but a dull one. One of the objects should dominate.

Arrangement and balance imply that you should not allow the photo to become top-heavy, bottom-heavy or allow objects to get clustered to one side. Make use of the whole picture area.

Some photographers, when photographing groups of objects, think of balance in terms of a triangular or pyramidal arrangement. Either of these forms is more pleasing to the eye than a random or shapeless mass.

One way to control balance and arrangement is by varying the camera distance and location. If you were to photograph a picnic table from one end at table top level, whatever objects happened to be in the foreground would dominate the scene, blocking out the objects at the other end. But if you got high above the table and shot down, all of the objects would be of equal importance.

Depth — Composition also concerns depth, the ability to impart a three-dimensional quality to your photos. Of course, every picture you take has some feeling of depth to it, but if you plan properly you can emphasize this quality, creating space and imparting the illusion of distance.

How does one create depth? Many ways. If you take a picture of a railroad track, the lines, although parallel, seem to converge as they approach the horizon, thus given a strong feeling of distance. Another example might be a row of columns, with the individual columns growing smaller and smaller as the distance increases. A road appears to come to a point at the horizon.

Another way to create a feeling of depth is by using a foreground object as point of visual contact. When you are photographing scen-

ery, for example, it's often effective to put a person in the foreground and at one side, perhaps admiring the view. This serves to emphasize the immensity of a landscape.

Foreground objects are also useful in framing the scene. A tree branch in the foreground, a fencepost or a rock formation can help to pull the composition together and enhance interest.

Opposite: Fence-line adds depth to this picture. (George Sullivan)

Below: Tree trunk and branches in the foreground heighten the feeling of depth here. (French Cultural Services)

Shadows can also be used to create a sense of depth. (Williamsburg Restoration, Inc.)

Shadows too are a way to create a sense of depth. Not only sun shadows but those created indoors by artificial lighting give greater perspective to the subject. Sometimes they can be used to improve the composition by leading the eye to the center of interest.

Last, there is a technical method you can use to increase depth. Focus on your central subject and then open the aperture (See Chapter 3). This puts the background slightly out of focus. It blurs it. This technique is often used when taking indoor photos and actual depth is limited.

Directional Lines — The linear arrangement of a photograph is much more important than most people realize. Often it has a profound emotional effect upon the impression the picture gives.

Vertical lines suggest strength and dignity. The composition has a soaring quality to it. The photograph of a towering cathedral cannot help but suggest power and lofty purpose.

84

Opposite: Strong vertical lines imply dignity, power. (George Sullivan)

The horizontal make-up of this picture gives a feeling of serenity. (U. S. Department of the Interior)

Horizontal lines impart a much different impression. They suggest tranquillity, perhaps because in our mind's eye we relate them to the human figure in repose. An interrupted view of Nebraska farmland stretching to the horizon, a long view of a tranquil ocean—scenes of this type with their dominating horizontal lines suggest stillness and calmness.

Diagonal lines often suggest movement. There's an active quality to the composition. Curving lines imply movement, too, but it is less impulsive, less violent. Curving lines give a feeling of gracefulness, of fluid action.

Use directional lines not only to impart movement and an emotional quality to your picture, but also to help you achieve balance. Use them to focus attention on your center of interest. Often such

Diagonal lines suggest movement; they add excitement. (George Sullivan)

lines are called leading lines. Footprints in the snow can be used to lead the eye to a lone hiker. The shoreline can direct the viewer's attention to a bather.

You can also use lines to frame your picture. Sometimes a doorway can be used in this fashion, a gatepost or a tree branch.

Lines of direction can also help you frame a subject. (George Sullivan)

L-shaped sections of cardboard are an aid to cropping. (George Sullivan)

Cropping — When you obtain an enlarged print, it's often possible to improve its composition by cropping. When you crop a photo you eliminate unwanted details, thereby strengthening the story you are seeking to tell.

Don't cut the picture to crop it; you may have second thoughts. Cut out two L-shaped pieces from a square of white cardboard. Lay them over the picture (see photo) so that they form a moveable border or frame. Keep adjusting the strips until the picture appears at its best.

You don't need a camera in your hands to practice the composition. Anytime you look at any scene, look for interesting angles, shapes and arrangements.

When you're sitting at your desk, visualize how the books, writing instruments and other objects might be arranged so as to create an interesting composition. You can do the same when you're seated at a table at home.

To sum up, composition amounts to planning. Never take the first picture that comes to mind. Study the scene. Observe every detail. What is the story you want to tell? How can you best tell it?

88

chapter 7

LIGHTING

Outdoors or indoors, the creative use of lighting is a vital element in getting good pictures. The sun—or its absence—can be used to create an infinite number of moods and effects.

The same is true when you work indoors. Available light, flash equipment, or floodlights and spotlights can be employed in a limitless variety of ways to produce distinctive photographs.

Sunlight

The sun is your most versatile source of light. Even though you don't have the slightest bit of control over it, you can learn to use it to your advantage.

The first thing you must do is to train yourself to see the sun as professional photographers see it. Learn to assess the direction and quality of light as you're planning your photographs.

As far as direction is concerned, there are four kinds—front lighting, 45 degree side lighting, 90 degree side lighting and back lighting. Each has its own catalog of advantages and disadvantages. Each can be used to created different special effects.

Front lighting is what you get on your subject when the sun

is directly at your back and striking the subject head-on. It varies, of course, with the position of the sun in the sky, but in general front lighting makes for a flat and toneless picture. Avoid it if possible.

Front lighting is particularly objectionable when the sun is near its zenith. This produces top lighting. If you attempt to take an outdoor portrait when the light is coming from directly overhead, you will find that undesirable shadows are produced under the subject's nose and chin.

In almost every case, you get far better results with 45 degree side lighting. This is encountered when the sun is 45 degrees to the left or right side of your camera, and about mid-way between the horizon and its zenith, that is, at midmorning or midafternoon. With 45 degree side lighting, the sun is bright enough to give photos a strong textural quality and at the same time it makes for dark shadowing which adds drama to the scene.

Side-lighting heightens dramatic effect. (George Sullivan)

Even greater dramatic effects are possible when the sun is at a 90 degree angle to your subject, that is, coming directly from one side. There is then a marked contrast between light and dark and the slightest variations in texture will be recorded. Really striking pictures are possible with 90 degree side lighting.

Back lighting, which occurs just before sunset or just after sunrise, means that you are facing the sun which is behind your subject. Long, tapering shadows will appear in the scene, giving a profound impression of depth. Exciting silhouettes, the subject rimmed in a thin band of light, are possible when there is back lighting.

Ninety-degree side-lighting brushes the highlights of this *terra cotta* decoration. (George Sullivan)

Back lighting gives a silhouette effect. (George Sullivan)

Getting proper exposure can be tricky, however, when the sun is in back of the subject. It's important to use a light meter. And you have to beware of stray light rays or glare entering the lens. A lens shade will usually remedy this.

The paragraphs above presuppose that you are taking pictures in bright sunlight, which assures strong contrasts. But clear skies and bright sun aren't available every day; in fact, depending on where you live and the time of the year, they can be something of a rarity.

There are definite limitations on the effects that you can create when the sun is masked by clouds or heavy smog. However, such conditions can be advantageous when it comes to portraits. With the sun barely shining through the cloud cover, the light is diffused and there are vague shadows. This gives a soft, warm quality to a portrait.

A gray day, one that is completely overcast, produces pictures that are dull and flat. When you must take pictures, it's wise to cut your exposure time by one full stop. This will increase picture contrast.

Indoor Lighting

There is a vast assortment of indoor photographs you can make—if you know the fundamentals of indoor lighting. There are three basic types of light used indoors. There is available light, sometimes called existing or natural light; there is the light provided by floodlights and there is flash equipment. Sometimes these are used singly and other times in combination.

Fast film and fast lenses make it possible for just about anyone to make pictures in all but the dimmest light. There is an immense convenience and a sense of freedom to available light, since there's no need to set up lights or bother with bulbs. And pictures taken

Light from a nearby window — available light—made this a distinctive photo. Subject is Richard Boone. (Wagner International Photos Inc.; Gary Wagner)

with available light often have great realism, a you-are-there quality.

But you should also know the fundamentals of artificial lighting. To professionals it's the very essense of indoor photography. However, each one of the different types of indoor light has its own special characteristics. The type you use depends on the particular picture situation and the conditions under which you're operating.

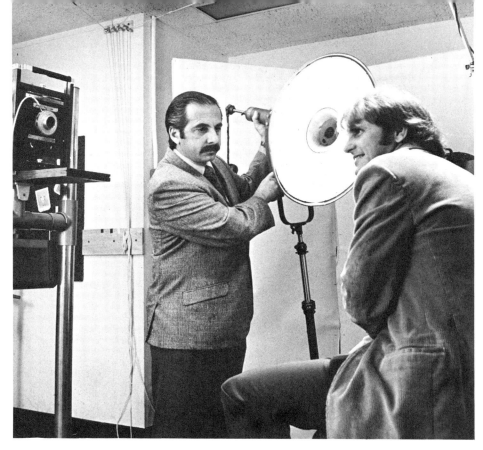

Floodlights are the most frequently used method of indoor lighting. (Wagner International Photos Inc.)

Floodlights — Floodlights, sometimes called photofloods or, simply, floods, are the most frequently used method of lighting an indoor scene. Inexpensive floodlights, the kind recommended for home use, resemble conventional household bulbs in that they are frosted, fit standard sockets and operate on home current of 110 volts. But the light they give is more intense, much more, while their life expectancy is far less. For example, a No. 1 photoflood resembles a 100-watt household bulb in size, but it produces the light of a 750-watt bulb and has a life span of about three hours.

94

Photofloods that resemble household bulbs in general appearance are meant to be used with silvery, bowl-shaped reflectors, which direct the light beam on the subject area. Professional photographers use photofloods which have a vaguely mushroom shape and a reflector lining, eliminating the need for a separate reflector.

How many floods you use, and how you arrange them, depends on your subject—whether it's a person or a bowl of fruit—and the effect you are seeking to create. But the advantage of this method of lighting is one of control. You can keep arranging and rearranging the lights until you get exactly what you want.

Suppose you're making a formal photograph of a person, a portrait. You can use virtually any room with light-colored walls as your studio. It should be large enough to enable you to set up your camera a distance of from 10–12 feet from the subject. You'll also need a backless seat for your subject, a stool or a bench, even a small box. Any of these is preferable to a chair, which encourages the subject to slump. Place the seat at least five feet from the wall, the background. This will help to give a feeling of depth to your picture.

What you want to do is arrange your lights so as to simulate the naturalness of sunlight or conditions of a well-lighted room. Yet there should be character in the way you light. If you're photographing a woman. you may want to soften the lighting to heighten her femininity.

You can use a basic two-lamp setup, a main light and a fill-in light. The main light should be set about four or five feet away from the subject and placed at about a 45 degree angle to the subject's left or right. Try the light on each side and choose the one that makes the subject more photogenic. Don't allow the light to create a shadow from the nose or brow across the subject's eyes. Usually this means you will have to direct the light downard at an angle of about 45 degrees.

A striking example of a well-lit portrait. TV's Ed Sullivan is the subject. (Wagner International Photos Inc.; Gary Wagner)

The second light should be set to the side of the camera which is opposite the main light (see diagram), and should be at about the subject's eye level. It should be a greater distance away than the main light. For instance, if the main light is four to five feet from the subject, the second light should be six to eight feet away.

This should be diffused light. Spread a piece of cheese cloth over the mouth of the reflector and secure it with a rubber band (or you can purchase a diffusion screen for this purpose). Be sure the cloth does not touch the bulb. The fill-in light balances the main light, subduing it, softening it.

Use a slow- or medium-speed film. A tripod is a necessity,

although you can set up your camera on a table or a chair, so long as you get the right height.

A shutter speed of 1/50 to 1/60 of a second is recommended. Use a *cable release*, a think flexible cord which attaches to the shutter release and allows you to make the exposure without any perceptible camera movement. Use a meter to determine the amount of exposure, taking a reading a distance of 6–12 inches from the subject's face.

If you plan to specialize in indoor photography, you will want to acquire additional lights and accessory equipment. Many photographers use a three-light setup in portrait work, using the third light as a background light or to raise the illumination level. It can also be used to accent and is sometimes placed in such a way that it emphasizes the hair of a woman or child.

Professional photographers also use such equipment as a *barn-door*, a pair of hinged flaps which are used to control the width of the beam of light. A *snoot*, a metal cone used to direct the beam to a small, specific area of the subject, is not uncommon. Professionals also make use of reflectors to brighten shadowed areas.

When it comes to lights themselves, however, there are limitations on the number you can use in your home, safety limitations, imposed by household wiring. Most home circuits are designed for maximum loads of 15 amperes, which means you cannot use much more than 1500 watts without blowing a fuse. If your photoflood setup includes two 500-watt and one 250-watt bulbs, you would be approaching the limit. It's always wise to disconnect conventional room lights and household appliances when you're using your floodlights, just to be on the safe side.

Keep in mind, however, the success of your indoor pictures doesn't depend on the amount of light you use. What's important is how the lighting is used and your skill in handling the camera. Used properly, a single floodlight is perfectly adequate for a home portrait.

A flash bulb setup (left) and electronic flash.

Flash — Flash is a second and equally versatile source of artificial light. There are two basic types: flash bulbs and electronic flash. Either one produces effects similar to those of floodlighting, but with the basic difference that the period of illumination is only a fraction of a second. The shutter action is synchronized to coincide with the peak intensity of the flash.

Why bother with flash? With fast film it's possible to make a picture under virtually any existing light condition. The answer has to do with control. With flash you can concentrate the light exactly where you want it, whereas with available light you have no such opportunity.

The element of control also applies to the quality of the light. With existing light, you seldom have the same quality twice, but flash always discharges the same amount of light. A photographer who always uses the same camera and flash setup is more likely to light and expose the picture correctly.

Another reason that flash is popular is that the intense light it produces enables you to use a small aperture for greater depth of field and high shutter speed to "freeze" action.

Flash bulbs differ in size and general appearance but they are all of the same basic construction. Each consists of a small, sealed bulb which has been coated with cellulose acetate to render it shatterproof. The bulb is filled with hair-fine flammable material and oxygen enough to assure instantaneous combustion. When you trip the shutter release, you send a surge of electricity into the bulb which ignites it.

In one type of flash illumination, the electric current to fire the bulb comes from a battery or a device known as a *battery-capacitor* (a B-C unit). In this, the batteries charge a capacitor which stores current. When you trip the shutter to fire the flash bulb, you also release current from the capacitor. It's a stronger, more dependable source of energy than the simple battery.

Professional photographers favor a second type of illumination—electronic flash. In this system, the bulb is actually a gas-filled tube which can be fired over and over again, as many as 10,000 times. This "bulb" is linked to one or more portable battery condensers where power is stored.

Electronic flash systems give illumination of extremely short duration. In portable units it's 1/500 to 1/2000 of a second, and it's even less with studio flash.

Whether you use electronic flash or flash bulbs depends chiefly on how often you are going to be using flash. Flash bulbs are recommended if you expect to take only a limited number of flash pictures. The initial cost of bulb equipment—the flash gun, reflector and the bulbs themselves—is much less than the cost of electronic flash equipment.

But if you're going to be shooting as many as 200 or 300 flash pictures over a year's time, electronic flash offers the greatest overall economy. There is also the matter of convenience. With electronic flash you do not have to be concerned with bulbs—buying them, storing them, loading them and disposing of them. And since electronic equipment provides flash of extremely brief duration, you can stop the fastest action with it.

Both the flash bulb system and electronic units can be used on the camera or off of it, that is, held at arm's length and to the right or left of the subject. This produces a shadowed area on one side of the subject and gives a feeling of depth to the picture.

Electronic flash—"bounce" flash, actually—was used in taking this portrait of actor Roddy McDowell. (Wagner International Photos Inc.; Gary Wagner)

A third method, one that is used to produce many different effects, involves the use of one or more flash *slave units*. These are usually of the battery-capacitor type, but they are not connected to the camera by wires. Instead, they are triggered electronically by the firing of the flash on the camera.

Flash equipment requires a much different working procedure than when shooting outdoors or using photofloods. You don't take a meter reading to determine exposure. You calculate exposure by guide numbers, charts of which accompany packaged flash bulbs and also film. Of course, these guide numbers are only approximate, and adjustments have to be made for such factors as the size of the room in which you're working and whether the walls are light or dark colored. (In general, you would increase exposure for a large room and dark-colored walls.)

Many of the points covered in the section on floodlights apply to flash photography. Where the light or lights are positioned is critical. You can place them to one side or above or below the subject. You can "bounce" them, that is point the flash toward a wall or other reflective surface to give soft, diffused lighting.

chapter 8

CAMERA CAREERS

Photography has so mushroomed in popularity in recent decades, that it is now a part of almost every phase of modern life. Thus, anyone seeking a career in photography can choose from a wide range of specialties.

There are photographers who limit themselves to industrial photographs or architectural subjects. There are those who specialize in photojournalism, portrait work or advertising photography. Photographers have become important to science and medicine. They are vital to the world of fashion.

What are the rewards of a career in photography? They're as varied as the specialties. For an industrial photographer, it may be the challenge of finding structural forms of beauty and excitement amidst what appears unattractive, even ugly. For the press photographer, it can be the excitement that comes with being a part of what's happening, plus the gratification of seeing one's work published and widely distributed within a matter of hours.

As for the financial rewards, there are photographers, a mere handful, it must be said, who receive as much as two thousand dollars for a single color photo, and whose annual income approaches six figures. At the other end of the scale, there is the neighborhood photographer to whom photography may be little more than a living.

How does one gain the experience necessary to become a professional photographer? The best way is by serving an apprenticeship, perhaps by working as an assistant to a professional photographer, or as a darkroom technician for a photo studio. If you're seeking a career in photojournalism, perhaps you will start as a staff photographer on a local newspaper.

Not every topnotch professional has had formal training in photography, but virtually all recommend it. It's the sound way to learn the fundamentals, *all* the fundamentals.

Introductory courses, usually once a week at night, are offered by public school adult education systems and private community agencies, such as the YMCA. A step up the ladder are photography schools or institutes. These are rather like private trade schools, offering students such advantages as knowledgeable instructors, well equipped laboratories and spacious studios. Fees can be high, however. Investigate thoroughly before you sign up.

It's even better to pursue your instruction at a two-year or a four-year college or university. Here you'll receive not only the technical training you require but also the all-embracing liberal arts schooling.

If you want more information about formal schooling, write to Photo Information, Eastman Kodak Company (343 State St., Rochester, N. Y. 14650) and ask for a free copy of "A Survey of Photographic Instruction." This is a comprehensive rundown of the educational programs offered by American schools of photography, technical institutions, colleges and universities.

Instruction is also available through correspondence courses. Beware here. Home-study courses can be unduly expensive, and they have the additional failing that you receive no direct supervision, nor is there opportunity to exchange ideas and information with fellow students.

It takes more than the usual amount of dedication to complete a home-study course. The dropout rate is enormous.

Don't decide to embark on a career in photography until you have a thorough understanding of what your preferred branch of the profession entails. A good way to get some solid information is to discuss your plans with someone already successful in the field, perhaps a local newspaper photographer, the head of a commercial photography studio, or perhaps the owner of an equipment shop.

Another wise plan is to seek out a trial job in the field. It could be a summer job with a photo finishing firm or part-time employment with a local newspaper. Weekly newspapers sometimes have opportunities for beginners.

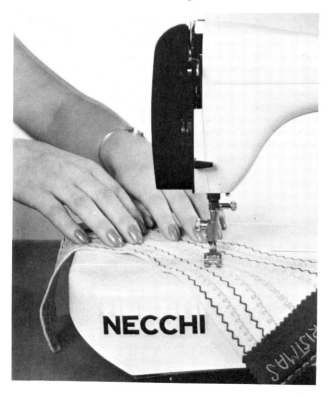

An advertising photograph has to convey the advertiser's message. (Wagner International Photos Inc.)

The principal career areas include the following:

Advertising Photography — The successful advertising photo is the one that sells the product or service. It must then communicate the advertiser's message. It takes ingenuity and imagination as well as superior technical skill to be able to achieve this.

Most specialists in this field are self-employed, that is, they are free-lance photographers who are hired by different advertising agencies when there is a need for their services. The agency art director is the man who does the hiring. He may interview many photographers for one assignment, studying carefully each man's portfolio of sample photos, before he makes his decision.

Once the photographer is hired, he and the art director plan the picture together. Often a detailed sketch is prepared showing what the photo is to look like. Props are ordered. Models are hired.

This is not a field for the novice. The best way to break into advertising photography is by serving an apprenticeship with a photographer or studio specializing in advertising art.

Fashion Photography — This is something of a branch of advertising photography, yet it demands a special range of skills. Besides imagination and technical ability, the fashion photographer must be a person of extreme sensitivity and often have a flair for the romantic. Richard Avedon, often adjudged to be the foremost of American Fashion photographers, is just as much an artist as he is a photographer.

Most fashion photographs are used either in advertising or to illustrate the pages of fashion magazines such as *Vogue* or *Harper's Bazaar*. Flip through one of these publications. Notice the dramatic quality of the photographs, the careful attention that has been given to staging and lighting.

There is no room for the beginner in fashion photography. The starting point is usually as an apprentice to someone well-established in the field.

Fashion photographs have an artistic quality. (Wagner International Photos Inc.)

Industrial Photography — The industrial photographer has to be extremely versatile. One day he may be asked to photograph a segment of his company's manufacturing or assembly processes, an assignment that involves elaborate lighting setups and challenges his imagination as he seeks to dramatize the ordinary. The next day he may be taking snapshots of babies for the employees' magazine.

106

The equipment he uses is likely to vary from a simple twin-lens reflex camera to all that is involved in shooting multiple exposures in color.

Industrial photography also embraces the scientific and technological study of machines and products. It includes the preparation of employee visual training aids—slides, filmstrips and motion pictures. Publicity photographs are often another responsibility of the industrial photographer.

Industrial photography offers special challenges. (Bethlehem Steel Corporation)

A small plant may have a one- or two-man department to handle its photographic needs, whereas an industrial giant, a firm like General Motors or the Ford Motor Company, will have photography departments in its plants throughout the country, and the total number of employees involved may be well up in the hundreds.

Industrial photography is a fast-growing field and one that offers opportunity for the newcomer. The starting job is often that of a darkroom assistant. Major industries also frequently use free-lance photographers.

One such free-lance is Arthur D'Arazien, long ranked as one of the most pre-eminent photographers in this field. He has performed assignments for U. S. Steel, Du Pont, General Electric and IBM, to name just a few. Some of the pictures he has made have been exhibited in the Metropolitan Museum of Art, evidence of the work of the industrial photographer often reflects the artistic.

Photojournalism — The photojournalist is not merely a photographer who records a news event. Not at all. He or she communicates impressions by creating an atmosphere or mood and advancing an interpretation.

It is not easy. Margaret Bourke-White, one of the first American photojournalists and one of the greatest, was the only American photographer in the Soviet Union during 1941, and she managed to get a meeting with Russian premier Joseph Stalin. "I made up my mind that I wouldn't leave without getting a picture of Stalin smiling," she once recalled. But at the meeting Stalin failed to show any emotion. His face was a mask.

"I got down on my hands and knees on the floor and tried out all kinds of postures searching for a good angle. Stalin looked down at the way I was squirming and writhing and in the space of a lightning flash he smiled—and I got my picture."

Sometimes the field of photojournalism is said to include press photography, work that involves the coverage of individual news

The photojournalist seeks to interpret news events, not merely capture them. Youngsters here were photographed during a New York City teachers' strike. (United Press International)

events or special interest features. But more and more the term is coming to refer exclusively to the photographer who performs assignments for the news or picture magazines. (Margaret Bourke-White was a *Life* staff member).

Most photojournalists are employed on a free-lance basis, selling their work to several different magazines. A young photographer interested in this field usually begins by offering his work to general newsstand publications, special interest publications or newspapers. He must carefully study the style of the publication and determine its wants before submitting anything. If his pictures are technically sound, if they tell a story or explain or interpret a situation, he will begin making sales. *Where and How to Sell Your Pictures* is the name of a helpful guidebook. Published by Amphoto (915 Broadway, New York, N. Y. 10010), it costs $2.50.

Another method is to use the services of a picture agency, a firm that sells the work of photographers for a percentage of the selling price (an amount that ranges from 40 to 60 per cent). Picture agencies are located in most large cities. They are listed in the "Yellow Pages" of metropolitan telephone directories under "Photographers' Agencies."

The American Society of Magazine Photographers (60 East 42nd St., New York, N. Y. 10017) has established picture rates for free-lancers. The fee for black-and-white photographs for magazines is "in no case less than $25 per photograph when purchased in a series."

Portrait Photography — To size up a person, his or her character, and then capture that on film—that's the essential task of the portrait photographer. More professionals specialize in this field than any other.

It takes enormous insight to be successful in this field, as well as technical skill and ingenuity. Yousuf Karsh of Ottawa is the most renowned portrait photographer of the day. Once, when he was photographing Sir Winston Churchill, the British leader refused to

110

Portrait photography requires special skills. (Wagner International Photos Inc.)

relinquish his perpetual cigar. Karsh stepped forward and boldly removed the cigar from Churchill's mouth. Other people in the room were stunned. Churchill glared—and Karsh clicked the shutter. The result was a photograph that has become a classic. It's one that reflects the indomitable British spirit, and there's a trace of belligerence there, too.

Portrait photographers maintain their own studios. The larger operations are staffed by several cameramen and a complete darkroom crew, including photo finishers, printers and specialists in retouching.

This field includes baby portraits, high school yearbook and graduation portraits, wedding portraits and business executive portraits. Despite the number and variety of types, most of the country's more than 20,000 photo studios take on other kinds of assignments to boost their income. Studio photographers cover weddings, conventions and business meetings, and some do legal photography, taking pictures for lawyers or insurance companies in connection with accident cases.

Aerial photography is burgeoning field (AT&T Photo Service)

These are the traditional fields of photography, but they do not represent all of the career areas by any means. There is photogrammetry—aerial photography—a field that has all but revolutionized mapping and map making. Highway planners and civil engineers rely on aerial cameramen, and they aid in tracking hurricanes and seeking out oil and other geological riches.

Architectural photography is still another specialty. It usually involves taking clear, well-lighted pictures of building exteriors, pictures that underscore the structure's character and form. There are also photographers who concentrate solely on architectural interiors.

112

Opposite: Some architectural photographers specialize solely in interiors. (French Cultural Services)

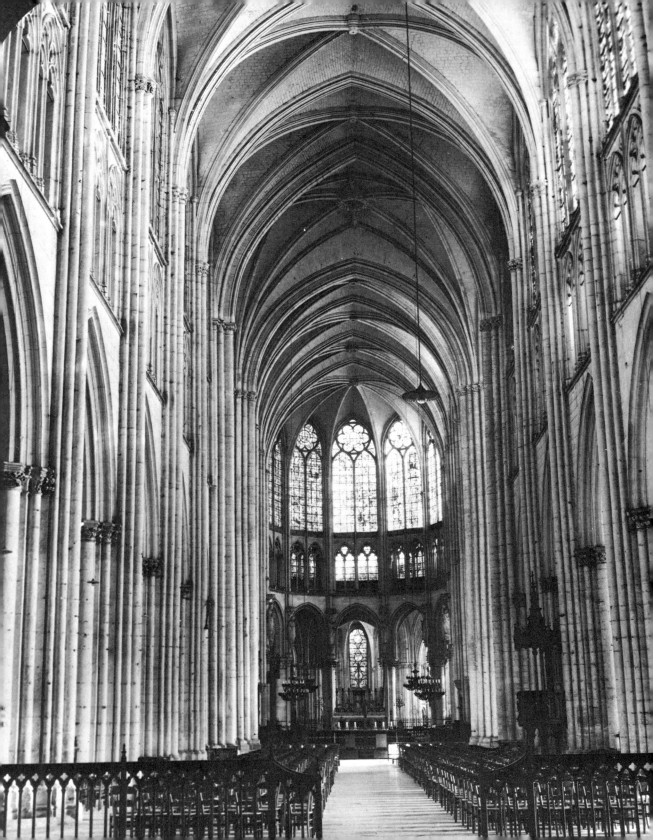

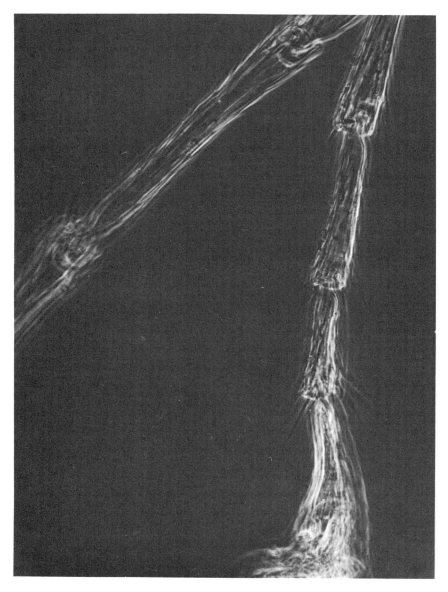

This is a photomicrograph—a photo taken through a microscope. The subject is the legs of an ant. (Margaret G. Cubberly, College of Physicians and Surgeons, Institute of Ophthalmology)

Medical photography, often called "bio-medical" because of its interrelation with the biological sciences, covers a wide range of activity. It includes clinical and surgical photographs and the field of photomicrography, photographing through a microscope.

Much of medical photography is educational in purpose, and involves the production of visual aids such as slides, filmstrips and motion pictures. As this implies, medical photographers are usually hospital or medical school staff members.

Not all careers in photography are in back of the camera. As photography grows in popularity, so does the need for laboratory personnel, for custom darkroom technicians and for color processors.

As the job descriptions in this section suggest, photography is often a glamorous field and sometimes an extremely exciting one. Like any field with these qualities, it is crowded and competitive. There is no quick and easy road to the top. But no successful photographer has ever said it isn't worth the climb.

Countless careers in photography involve laboratory work. (Wagner International Photos Inc.)

GLOSSARY

Aperture The tiny opening in the lens system through which light passes. The aperture size is regulated by the iris diaphragm which is calibrated in *f*-numbers. The larger the *f*-number, the smaller the aperture.

Barndoor A pair of hinged metal flaps used to control the width of the beam of light from a floodlight.

Battery capacitor In flash photography, an element in the electrical circuit which stores the charge temporarily and releases it to the flash bulb when the shutter is tripped.

Cable release A thin, flexible cord, fitted at one end with a small plunger, which attaches to the shutter release to enable you to make the exposure with a minimum of camera movement.

Camera obscura Literally a "darkened chamber" in which the image of an object is received through a small opening and focused onto a facing surface.

Crop To eliminate part of a print in order to improve the composition of the picture or exclude undesired features.

Depth of field The area, both before and behind the point of principal focus, in which all objects are in sharp focus.

Development The process by which a visible image is produced or an exposed piece of film from the latent image left on the film after exposure to light.

Diaphragm (iris diaphragm) The device used for adjusting the lens aperture. It consists of a series of thin metal leaves arranged in circular fashion which can be adjusted to enlarge or contract, thus varying the size of the aperture.

Emulsion The light sensitive coating, consisting of tiny grains of silver in a thin, gelatin layer, on photographic film.

Enlarger (photo-enlarger) In printing, a device used to optically magnify the negative from which a print is to be made.

Exposure The lens aperture and the shutter time used in taking a picture.

Exposure Meter A photoelectric instrument that measures light intensity in a given area and indicates the proper exposure for each of several shutter speeds.

f-**numbers** The system used to express the size of the lens aperture.

Fixer (fixing bath) In printing, the solution which makes permanent on film or paper the image brought out in development.

Flash bulb A small sealed glass bulb filled with oxygen and a hair-fine flammable material which is ignited by an electric charge to produce a short-duration, high intensity light flash.

Focal Length The distance from the lens to the film when the camera is focused on its "infinity" mark. Focal length is measured in millimeters, as in 35 mm lens, 400 mm, etc.

Hypo (short for **hyposulfite**) See fixer. Consists of sodium hyposulfite plus an acid.

Image An optical reproduction of an object formed by a lens.

118

Iris diaphragm   See diaphragm.

Lens   A small disk of optical glass by means of which rays of light are focused as they pass through it.

Lens System   Several elements of selected optical glass fixed in a tubular arrangement to act as a single lens.

Negative   Exposed film on which the tone values are reversed from the subject photographed.

Overexposure   A condition that results when too much light has been given to the film. An overexposed negative is black, almost opaque. A print made from the negative is the reverse—chalk white and lacking in any detail.

Parallax   A condition that results when the viewfinder and lens of a camera are separated; in close-ups, what one sees in the finder is likely to be different from what appears on the film.

Print   A photographic image made by passing light through a negative onto sensitized paper.

Printing   The process by which a picture is produced from a negative.

Safelight   A lamp with one or more color filters capable of permitting moderate darkroom illumination without exposing light sensitive film or paper.

Shutter   A mechanical device which opens and shuts the lens aperture.

Slave unit   In flash photography, a battery capacitor, electronic flash unit that is triggered by the firing of a flash unit on the camera.

Snapshot   A picture taken in a perfunctory manner, without thought or careful preparation.

Snoot A black, metal cone used to spot the beam from a floodlight onto a small, specific area.

Speed In connection with a lens, its light transmitting ability. Lens speed is measured in terms of the size of the largest possible aperture, which is expressed by an f-number, as $f/1.2$, or $f/3.5$, etc.

Underexposure A condition that results when insufficient light has been given to the film. An underexposed negative lacks in detail or may be almost completely transparent. A print made from the negative will be the reverse—dark, tending toward opacity.

Viewfinder (finder) A device on the camera that indicates to the photographer what appears in the field of view of the lens.

BIBLIOGRAPHY

For additional reading:

BRUCE, HELEN FINN. *Your Guide to Photography*. New York: Barnes & Noble, Inc., 1971.

The Camera, by the editors of Time-Life Books. New York, 1970.

CHERNOFF, GEORGE and SARBIN, HERSHEL. *Photography and the Law*. New York: Amphoto, 1958.

CROY, OTTO R. *The Complete Art of Printing and Enlarging*. Philadelphia: Chilton Book Co., 1969.

DESCHIN, JOSEPH. *Photography in Your Future*. New York: The Macmillan Co., 1965.

EISENSTAEDT, ALFRED and GOLDSMITH, ARTHUR. *The Eye of Eisenstaedt*. New York: The Viking Press, 1969.

EPSTEIN, SAMUEL and DEARMAND, DAVID. *How to Develop, Print and Enlarge Pictures*. New York: Grosset & Dunlap, 1970.

FENTON, D. X. *Better Photography for Amateurs*. New York: Amphoto, 1970.

121

FORSEE, AYLESA. *Famous Photographers*. Philadelphia: Macrae Smith, Co., 1968.

GERNSHEIM, HELMUT and ALISON. *A Concise History of Photography*. New York: Grosset & Dunlap, 1965.

GERMAR, HERB. *The Student Journalist and Photojournalism*. New York: Richards Rosen Press, 1967.

KINNE, RUSS. *The Complete Book of Nature Photography*. Philadelphia: Chilton Book Co., 1971.

MORGAN, WILLARD, Editor. *The Encyclopedia of Photography*. New York: Greystone Press, 1964.

NEBLETTE, C. B. *Photography, Its Materials and Processes*. Princeton, N.J.: D. Van Nostrand, Co., 1966.

NEWHALL, BEAUMONT. *Airborne Camera: The World from the Air and Outer Space*. New York: Hastings House, 1969.

PAYNE, LEE. *Getting Started in Photojournalism*. Philadelphia: Chilton Book Co., 1967.

The Print, by the editors of Time-Life Books. New York, 1970.

RHODE, ROBERT B. *Introduction to Photography*. New York: The Macmillan Co., 1971.

SCHWARZ, THEODORE. *The Business Side of Photography*. New York: Amphoto, 1969.

Amphoto (915 Broadway, New York, N.Y. 10010), the leading publisher of books about photography, has available a catalog listing 600 different titles. These books are in every price range and cover the field from all aspects. The catalog is free. Write and request one.

INDEX

Viewing system 46, 47, 53
Vogue Magazine 105

W

Wedgwood, Thomas 15
Wet-plate process 16, 18

White light 28, 29
Wide-angle lens 59, 60

Y

Yashica Camera 51
Y.M.C.A. 103